D0443245

EMPIRE OF FREEDOM

EMPIRE OF FREEDOM

The Amway Story
and What It Means to You

JAMES W. ROBINSON

Foreword by Richard L. Lesher

PRIMA PUBLISHING

© 1997 by James W. Robinson

All rights reserved. No part of this book may be reproduced or transmitted in any form or by any means, electronic or mechanical, including photocopying, recording, or by any information storage or retrieval system, without written permission from Prima Publishing, except for the inclusion of quotations in a review.

PRIMA PUBLISHING and colophon are registered trademarks of Prima Communications, Inc.

Library of Congress Cataloging-in-Publication Data

Robinson, James W.
Empire of freedom : the Amway story and what it means to you/James W. Robinson; foreword by Richard L. Lesher.
   p. cm.
Includes bibliographical references.
ISBN 0-7615-0675-6
   1. Amway Corporation. 2. Direct selling. I. Title.
HF5439.H82R63 1996
381'.13'0973—dc20   96-28993
                                         CIP

96 97 98 99 HH 10 9 8 7 6 5 4 3 2 1
Printed in the United States of America

How to Order:
Single copies may be ordered from Prima Publishing, P.O. Box 1260BK, Rocklin, CA 95677; telephone (916) 632-4400. Quantity discounts are also available. On your letterhead, include information concerning the intended use of the books and the number of books you wish to purchase.

Visit us online at http://www.primapublishing.com

Contents

Foreword

The growth of Amway—from a rural, small-town basement operation in 1959 to a multibillion-dollar global phenomenon involving 2.5 million people in more than 70 countries and territories—is one of America's most spectacular business success stories. But it is much more than that. The Amway story vividly and powerfully reminds us all that the values we hold dear—freedom, private enterprise, individual initiative, personal responsibility, and the love of family—are universal in scope and appeal. Once unleashed, they are unbeatable and unstoppable in any country or culture.

Should it really surprise us that when Amway opens its doors in a country recently freed from the yoke of socialism, hopeful people by the tens of thousands virtually beat down the doors to get in? Amway's winning formula of placing a low-cost business opportunity in the hands of average people, and thus giving them a means to pursue their dreams, appeals to qualities that are not simply uniquely American, but uniquely human.

It didn't start out that way. Amway began quite simply when two young men with limited means set out to find a better way to feed their families. They ended up creating a business that now feeds millions of families.

Today, as the preeminent direct sales organization, Amway is a leading force in a potent economic, social, and political movement that is fundamentally changing our country. Aided by cheap, but powerful, user-friendly communications and information technology, the ranks of the self-employed and of small, family-owned enterprises are swelling rapidly. As I conclude in my own recent book, *Meltdown on Main Street*, the small business revolution is here to stay and will have a decisive influence on our economy and our political process for years to come. Amway is in the vanguard of that revolution.

Amway's rapid corporate expansion, its impact on the global economy, and its role in changing the way consumers buy everyday products all make for a fascinating story. More important, the Amway story is a story about people. From top to bottom, from start to finish, the character of this company is defined by the quality of the people in it.

I have known founders Rich DeVos and Jay Van Andel for more than 20 years, personally and professionally. Unlike some highly successful, wealthy people, the more you get to know Rich and Jay the more you like and respect them. When you think of them, you immediately think of words like integrity, loyalty, devotion to family, and courage to take a stand—be it in business, politics, or life, and never mind the criticism or the consequences!

When Rich and Jay say this business is great for families, they mean it. Amway has always been a family affair for the DeVoses and the Van Andels. All eight of their children are deeply involved in steering the company into the next century. When Rich and Jay say this business is all about helping others succeed as you succeed, they mean that too. Their friendship and partnership has lasted, solid as a rock, for more than 50 years. How many other high-profile partnerships—especially in the world of big business—can you think of that have lasted that long? From time to time, some have tried to drive a wedge between them. It never happened. It never will.

The author of this book, Jim Robinson, was "just a kid" when he came to work for me at the U.S. Chamber of Commerce in the early 1980s. Just a kid—who had already done some writing for Ronald Reagan and important members of Congress. From the beginning, I was impressed by Jim's devotion to the free enterprise system and his desire to use his facility with words to advance the principles upon which both America and the Chamber were founded.

Since then, Jim has advised some of our country's most prominent government and business leaders. In the late 1980s, the governor of California asked him to develop an international business plan for the Golden State and establish a network of five California trade offices overseas. He has written five books before this one, covering topics such as business communications, politics, and commercial opportunities in Vietnam. He is the ideal person to tell the Amway story as the company enters a new and exciting chapter as a global phenomenon that is positively improving people's lives in over 70 countries.

Whether you are in the Amway business or in any business—whether you have reached the personal pinnacles toward which you have striven or are hungering for a new beginning—I commend this book to you. It's a remarkable story, remarkably told, a story of common people achieving uncommon things every day and, in the process, changing the world for the better.

Richard L. Lesher
President, U. S. Chamber of Commerce

Acknowledgments

Help comes in a variety of forms when one is writing a book. I thank all those who supported this effort in a dozen different ways and helped me see it through.

Basil Halabi proved to be not only a devoted friend but a creative, skillful, and dedicated researcher. Ben and Nancy Dominitz guided and inspired me every step of the way.

Thanks also to:

Jim Dornan, Jim Elliott, Jim Floor, Brian Hays, Pat and Betty Kaufmann, Frank Morales, Willy Victor, Dan and Bunny Williams, and many other leaders in Amway who gave of their time and their wisdom to help me get it right.

Tom Donohue and Dick Lesher for their guidance and for continuing to challenge me personally and professionally.

Kim Bruyan and Beth Dornan at Amway Corporation.

Karen Blanco, Steven Martin, Susan Silva, and Jennifer Basye Sander at Prima.

To the many quiet heroes in Amway who spoke to me in person, by phone, or through tape. There are too many to mention here, but I hope my treatment of your stories and experiences in this book demonstrates my gratitude.

Thanks also to Toni Green, Suzie Matthews, and my colleagues at ATA.

And to Duc and Dagny for always being there. You always will be.

Note to the Reader

This book is an account of an extraordinary business movement that helps people believe in their ability to do great things through free enterprise.

Amway is accurately called several things: a direct-selling business, a network marketing business, and a multilevel marketing business.

Fundamentally, Amway is a leadership business. It's all about people. So to tell this story, I set out to talk to as many leaders in the business as my time, and theirs, would allow. I also drew information and inspiration from the excellent written accounts that have appeared in the past, books such as Rich DeVos's *Compassionate Capitalism*.

Meeting these successful and optimistic people has been an enriching experience. I could have easily spent one more year, even two more years, just meeting the people of Amway. But this is a story that urgently needs to be told. There is so much negativism out there, not just about Amway, but about life. So we had to balance the desire to include more people in the book with the need to tell a story I believe many are hungering to hear today.

To the many great Amway leaders, I say: If I was able to talk to you and include you and your organization in the book, thank you for sharing a bit of your lives with me. If I was not, please understand that it is no reflection on your achievements or on those of your organization. I look forward to meeting you soon!

What is most important is that we set the record straight about this wonderful business and spread its message of hope to as many people as possible. That mission, I'm sure you'll agree, transcends any concerns about who is mentioned in the book and who is not. As the saying goes, "A rising tide lifts all boats." There is only one Amway Plan!

To those not in the Amway business, I'd like you to understand that for every story told in this book, there are 10, 50, 100 stories that are untold. That's the power of this business. The people who share their lives with you in the following pages were chosen not for who they are but for what they represent. I hope they will enrich your lives as they have enriched mine.

James W. Robinson

1

Voyage of Discovery

To millions of people in the world Amway would appear just as you think it is. A crazy idea.
—Rich DeVos

"I have a question for *you.*" I was a little taken aback by Pat Kaufmann's direct manner. Pat and his wife, Betty, are nationally recognized leaders in the Amway business, having achieved the level of Executive Diamond Direct Distributors in the International Connection organization. I was interviewing them for my book about this $6.3 billion phenomenon and *I* was supposed to be the one asking the questions.

"Sure, Pat," I replied. "Go ahead."

"How can it be that you, a middle-aged adult, have never heard of Amway? You've never crossed paths with Amway before?"

How else could I respond? "That's a good question," I answered. "A very good question."

After all, I had served in high positions in business and government. I had written speeches for congressmen, presidential candidates, governors, and national political conventions. I had helped shape business policies and international trade strategies for the "nation-state" of

California. I'd established foreign offices in Hong Kong, Japan, and Mexico City, and I had written a book on the emerging market of Vietnam.

But I knew nothing about Amway, and no one had ever approached me about it. In all those circles in which I worked and traveled, I had never known a single Amway distributor. Clearly, as big as the business has become, large segments of the professional world have yet to be introduced to Amway.

To be totally accurate, I had met one man involved in the Amway business. It was in 1981, and I was brand new in my speechwriting job at the U.S. Chamber of Commerce in Washington, D.C. One of the first meetings I attended was a gathering of the Chamber's board of directors, and an impressive, charismatic man who reminded me of Jimmy Stewart and Billy Graham all mixed together got up to speak. Boy, could he speak! Beautiful, inspiring words about America and free enterprise. I went up to him afterward and introduced myself.

He was Jay Van Andel, cofounder of Amway. I loved his words. I knew he was important. But I really had no idea what he did for a living.

Despite Pat Kaufmann's chagrin, the fact that I had never been approached about joining the business has probably not been much of a loss for Amway. But I now realize it has been a great loss for me. Let me tell you why.

In the course of my career in politics and business, my job has been to sell the principles of free enterprise and limited government, the only form of government truly compatible with free enterprise. I did my job pretty well and believed passionately in what I was doing. Now, what is one of the first things Amway sponsors teach their new distributors? You've got to know the products. You've got to use the products.

Not me. I sold free enterprise to others while most of the time collecting a government paycheck for myself. It was a product I didn't use and didn't really know.

I found that out the hard way.

In late 1990, California governor George Deukmejian was wrapping up eight successful years in Sacramento. I had served on his personal staff from the beginning. Both of us—and many others in his administration—now faced the prospect of starting a new chapter in private life.

The governor was excited by the challenge. He had served Californians honorably in various offices for a total of 28 years. Unlike many others in politics, he maintained no business or income on the side. Now he was ready voluntarily to give up the trappings of power for the promise of drumming up clients and practicing law for a law firm in Los Angeles.

I thought I was ready too. I turned down a big corporate communications job on the East Coast, one that would pay more money than I had ever dreamed of making in my life. I turned it down so that I could strike out on my own and open my own public relations and public affairs shop. The plan seemed pretty simple. With a former governor as my first client (for whom I would continue to write speeches, handle media inquiries, and help line up speaking engagements), I would build a business around my considerable contacts in California government and media.

Presenting my idea to Governor Deukmejian in the closing months of the administration, I remember his words well: "Go for it. This is your chance to actually live the life you've been writing about and trying to convince others to lead—the life of an independent entrepreneur, not dependent on government, only yourself."

I flopped. And I've got a dozen excuses to explain why. The economy turned bad. People made promises to me they didn't keep. I didn't have enough staff support. My ongoing work for the ex-governor took too much time. Within nine months, I was back in government, at a lower-level position and making less money than I had made in the governor's office!

I spent a long time trying to figure out what went wrong. Why was I so poorly equipped to live, and not just preach, the principles of private enterprise in which I believed so strongly? It wasn't until I got to know the people of Amway and hear their stories that I finally figured it out. It all came down to this: I was scared. I lacked self-confidence. I feared rejection. And I was incapable of developing a plan for success. I asked for no one's help because I thought that being an entrepreneur meant you had to do it all alone.

It seems so clear now. I was so used to having big, powerful CEOs and lobbyists knocking on my door. I couldn't imagine having to knock on theirs. It made me ashamed. I actually found myself dialing numbers of former associates and contacts to seek business so that I'd be off the hook—at least for another day!

When I placed cold calls I prayed for voice mail so I could delay for just one more hour, one more day, the possibility of another rejection! How I could have benefited from the encouragement of Mitch and Deidre Sala, Amway Triple Diamond Direct Distributors from Australia. While building their Amway business, they became experts on the subject of rejection.

"I want you to think of us whenever things are going badly," Mitch likes to tell distributors just starting out in the Amway business. When *they* were starting out, they experienced 42 rejections in a row from prospects. Instead of throwing in the towel, they became all the more determined to succeed. "I felt like asking the people who turned us down, 'What's the matter with you? Don't you love your children?' [Instead,] we simply decided to do whatever it would take to succeed."

And they have. Mitch and Deidre Sala today lead one of Amway Australia's most thriving lines of sponsorship.

* * *

All of this was running rapidly through my mind as I drove east on Fulton Road out of Grand Rapids and into the hilly green countryside of rural Michigan. I quickly began to wonder if I had made a wrong turn. I had flown into Kent County Airport earlier that day and saw nothing but dairy farms as the plane approached and landed. Now, I was really perplexed. There couldn't possibly be a multi-billion-dollar business operating in more than 70 countries and territories tucked away in this pastoral setting.

Suddenly, I reached the crest of the next hill, and I could see it: a city unto itself. One-and-two-tenths miles of offices, factories, warehouses, shipping docks, and parking lots—a beehive of activity. Big rigs full of freshly manufactured and packaged products pulling out; bus-loads of brand new Direct Distributors arriving for seminars, their faces bright with hope and their voices full of anticipation.

I was at Amway world headquarters in Ada, Michigan—the nerve center of one of the largest direct-selling companies in America and the twenty-second largest privately held company in the country. With 2.5 million independent distributors selling its products around the globe, Amway's estimated retail sales soared to $6.3 billion in its fiscal year ending in August 1995—a 19 percent increase over the prior year and 12,600 times the level of sales in 1960, the company's first full year of operation.

Supporting this global sales reach are over 450 scientists and other professional staff members working in 57 research and development laboratories. The company holds more than 100 patents on products worldwide and maintains 10 million square feet of facilities staffed by 13,000 employees. Amway operates in more than 70 countries and territories, opening 20 new affiliates since 1990 alone.

Reflecting on such astounding growth, I pulled off the road and gazed upon the headquarters complex. What was really behind such spectacular success? What explained it? And how could it happen in the face of all the negativism surrounding both Amway and other direct-selling companies?

I came face to face with such negativism while writing this book. I can't count the number of times that friends and professional associates, when learning of my topic, groaned and said, "Oh no, Jim, you must be kidding!" Interestingly, not one of them had ever been part of the business.

All of these reactions filled my mind as I parked on the shoulder of Fulton Road that warm summer day. And then I thought about a scene Jim Dornan witnessed recently on the other side of the world. As the founder and president of Network 21, one of the largest organizations of Amway distributors, Jim's leadership has been instrumental in fueling the phenomenal growth of Amway in international markets from Southeast Asia to Latin America to Eastern Europe. He won't admit it or talk about it himself, but the fact is that in many of those burgeoning markets, Jim Dornan, along with his wife, Nancy, are not only household names, but they have also reached hero status in many quarters.

"Thanks to pioneers like Robert Angkasa and Paul and Linda Agus, Network 21 has a significant portion of the Amway business in Indonesia, one of the most populous countries in the world," Jim told me recently.

"One of our downline distributors, S. R. Kristiawan, was a 24-year-old college student and kind of the black sheep of his family when his father first introduced him to the Amway Sales and Marketing Plan. He was so excited. Back at college, he went to work signing up people. His first Network 21 weekend seminar was attended by 2,500 people. Six months later, he brought 2,500 of his own people to a rally where Nancy and I spoke. You won't believe this, but more than 7,000 Indonesians filled that stadium.

"The reception we received was unbelievable. The cheers, the enthusiasm. It was an interesting sight to see women of the Muslim faith dressed in their traditional clothing, arms stretched upward, whooping and hollering along with everyone else.

"Then it started to rain. I mean it was a torrential downpour. The speakers were lucky—the stage was covered. But the audience was not. They sat, stood, listened, and cheered in this driving, monsoon-like rain. All 7,000. I didn't see anyone leave!"

Today, S. R. Kristiawan has more than 50,000 distributors in his group.

I thought of that torrential Indonesian downpour as I gazed upon the Michigan dream factory down the road. Then, the answer to my question came to me with simple clarity. As good as they are, the products, the plan, and the corporate strategies don't adequately explain Amway's success around the world and its potency as a global force for positive change. It's really all about *people*—and it all started with two.

* * *

A "crazy idea"? It sure seemed that way back in 1959 when Rich DeVos and Jay Van Andel started their new company literally at the ground level—in the basements of the DeVos and Van Andel family homes in the predominately Dutch-American community of Ada, Michigan.

Rich and Jay, as they were and are commonly known, had already been close friends, business partners, and fellow adventurers for nearly 20 years. They date the beginning of their association, which now spans more than a half century, to when Jay was 16 and Rich 14. Jay had just been given an old Ford Model A by his father but had little money for gas. Rich needed a ride to the high school they both attended but had no transportation. He paid Jay 25 cents a week for gas, and thus one of the world's most successful and endurable partnerships was born.

Their friendship deepened. They shared ideas and youthful adventures. As a son and grandson of immigrants and children of the Great Depression, they were profoundly motivated by the desire to achieve economic independence and self-sufficiency. Like so many others, they had to find a way to do this with virtually no start-up money.

"There had to be another way for people like us, who wanted a business of our own, to get started," DeVos later wrote. "Here we had a knack for sales and plenty of ambition, but we certainly didn't begin to have the capital resources needed to carve out our niche in the precarious marketplace we now pictured."

That dream was deferred as the two young men entered military service. Jay became a commissioned officer in the Air Force; Rich joined the Army Air Corps. Their postings pulled Rich and Jay apart for several years, but their planning and dreaming through the mailbox continued uninterrupted.

Their experiences in military aviation convinced them that there was money to be made from America's new love affair with the world of flight. So when they returned to Michigan, they decided to test this perception and capitalize on their experience by starting their first venture, a flying school called Wolverine Air Service. They purchased a small plane for $700 and hired an instructor for it while they focused on recruiting students. A drive-in hamburger stand and a small shop that sold accessories to students quickly followed.

Rich and Jay's early ventures were reasonably successful, but the partners quickly began to question their long-term potential for growth. So they sold the businesses and began to search anew. But first they set out on what proved to be a madcap adventure. Deciding they wanted to sail for South America, the friends purchased a 38-foot schooner and set out for the Caribbean.

They made it to the coast of Cuba, where their boat sprung a leak—lots of leaks! They were rescued by a passing vessel.

Refusing to return home in failure, the adventurers worked their way by land, sea, and air until they reached Buenos Aires. They returned home to great local interest in their story and gained considerable practice in the art of speechmaking and presentation as they recounted their escapades to eager audiences.

Turning their sights back to the business world, Jay and Rich formed a company appropriately called the Ja-Ri Corporation. The only problem was that they weren't really sure what products they wanted to sell or how. They were still searching for a winning formula.

The turning point came in 1949, when Jay's second cousin, a man named Neal Maaskant, told the pair about a business he had entered selling a nutritional food supplement product for a company called Nutrilite. Nutrilite had been founded by Carl Rehnborg, who, as a prisoner in a Chinese detention camp in the 1920s, survived by eating cooked plants and animal bone. Rehnborg later returned to the United States with a strong belief in the health benefits of vitamins and nutritional supplements. In starting Nutrilite, he was not only an early pioneer in the health and fitness craze but in many respects the founding father of direct selling.

Not only did the Nutrilite products have a somewhat captivating allure, but the company also had a unique marketing approach. Distributors sold the supplements directly to consumers. They earned income from those sales as well as from the sales of other distributors they recruited.

Rich and Jay were quickly convinced that this was the winning formula. They invested $49 for a sales kit and some products and set out to recruit distributors, drawing on the presentation skills they had honed after their return from South America. Within the first year they grossed $82,000; they increased that sum fourfold the very next year. Soon, they had built one of the most successful Nutrilite distributorships in America.

Business and personal growth continued through the 1950s, with Rich and Jay both starting families. By 1958, however, internal conflicts within Nutrilite's management prompted the pair, along with the major distributors in their organization, to develop their own distinct organization and line of products while still selling Nutrilite products. The American Way Association was established that year and Amway Corporation the following year, setting up shop in the basements of the DeVos and Van Andel homes.

In 1959, Jay and Rich purchased the rights to an innovative all-purpose cleaner that was concentrated and kind to the environment. Today, L.O.C. (Liquid Organic Cleaner) is still fondly and proudly listed as product number one in Amway's now extensive catalog of offerings to consumers.

With a quality product and a business plan that put the dream of a better life in the hands of average people, Rich DeVos and Jay Van Andel and the company they founded began their meteoric rise.

Today, the dream of building one's own business is a fervent mission that is attracting millions of people from different walks of life all over the world and reshaping the global economy in a fundamental way. Amway is in the vanguard of this movement.

We'll explore this and many other important and fascinating issues in this book:

- Why owning your own business has become the lifestyle of choice in the 1990s
- What makes Amway grow so fast, particularly in the international arena
- How technology has greatly increased your chances for success as an independent business owner
- Why the self-employed are the fastest-growing group of workers in our economy
- Why Amway appeals to such a diversity of people—from affluent doctors and lawyers in the United States and Canada to housewives in Japan and factory workers in Poland
- How Amway has succeeded in cracking open tough foreign markets when so many others have failed
- How many people *really* make it in Amway (and the industry alternatively known as direct selling, multilevel marketing, and network marketing)
- How much it costs to get started
- Why small business owners are becoming such a powerful agent for political and social change
- How you can build and run a multinational business from your basement or den, just as Rich DeVos and Jay Van Andel did

But most important, we're going to reveal the true nature of this often maligned and misunderstood business. (Please understand, I have reached my conclusions independently. I am not an Amway distributor, nor do I derive any compensation from Amway Corporation.)

Before I began writing this book, I, like most people, did not fully appreciate how Amway is transforming the lives of millions of men and women across the globe— and, in the process, revolutionizing the business world. Now, however, having interviewed countless Amway distributors, I understand why thousands of people would sit riveted through a monsoon just to learn about the opportunities Amway offers.

In this book, we'll explore how and why Amway has been able to change so many lives for the better in ways extending far beyond business. Some have become rich in Amway. So many more have become *enriched.*

2

Best of Times,
Worst of Times

By most objective standards, the last half century in our national life has been enormously successful. Americans have achieved unprecedented levels of material prosperity and personal freedom. We are healthier, work at less exhausting jobs, and live longer than at any time in our history.
　　　　—Robert J. Samuelson, economist

They can call it reengineering, downsizing, restructuring, but it still means you are fired.
　　　　—Middle manager, dismissed after 25 years
　　　　with his company

Being laid off never crossed Don and Sherry Marshall's minds when they started their Amway business eight years ago. These Colorado residents were instead attracted by the environmental attributes of the products and the prospect of earning some extra income.

But the very month the Marshalls became Direct Distributors, an important milestone in the Amway business, they both lost their jobs at the company where Don had put in 18 years and Sherry 8 years. If it were not for their Amway business, says Don, "we may have lost everything."

Ron and Georgia Lee Puryear nearly did. Back in the late 1960s, when the American economy was still running on high octane, Ron suffered a calamity that ominously foreshadowed the dislocations of the present day. He was an accountant at a privately owned nuclear power facility in Washington State. "I had advanced through the ranks and held a responsible middle-management position," Ron told Rich DeVos in the Amway cofounder's 1993 book, *Compassionate Capitalism.*

Ron said: "All my life I had been taught that success and security would come if I got a good education, found a good job, and worked hard at it. That morning, as I drove to my parking place in that giant nuclear-research facility, I was convinced that I had paid my dues and found the American dream."

That dream turned into a nightmare when Ron arrived at his desk and found an envelope. Inside was a letter telling him that his services, along with those of 2,100 of his coworkers, would no longer be required. His employer had lost its government contract.

The ensuing months were filled with rejection, as Ron made all the rounds in search of another job. When he finally got one, he made 30 percent less money and worked twice as many hours as he had before.

Unemployment and then a pay cut were hard on the Puryear family's finances. Georgia Lee had always vowed she would be there for the couple's two children when they got home from school. Now she was forced out of the house and into a job as a waitress at a Denny's restaurant. "Neither of us liked what we were doing," Georgia Lee recalls. "We hardly saw each other, let alone our children. We were tired most of the time. Our tempers were often short."

Life works in mysterious ways. In the Puryears' case, the fact that some friends showed them a new business opportunity at the precise time when they were the most unhappy and dissatisfied set them on a course that changed their lives forever. "If they had called at any other time in our lives," Georgia Lee says, "we probably would not have listened."

That business opportunity was Amway. The next time Ron left his job, it was not because he was fired but because he quit. "I chose freedom," he says.

Today, Triple Diamonds Ron and Georgia Lee Puryear and their World Wide Dreambuilders organization help tens of thousands of people free themselves from both the fear and the reality of economic calamity.

A NEW REALITY

"They were the best of times. They were the worst of times." Charles Dickens' immortal line fits our times today.

There is much to be thankful for and hopeful about. In the United States, unemployment and inflation are low and the country is at peace. The Cold War has been won. Democracy and free enterprise are taking root, from Eastern Europe to Latin America to Southeast Asia. The world goes to sleep at night without the fear of nuclear annihilation—something few dreamed possible just a few years ago.

But if things are so good, why don't we feel so good?

Economist Robert J. Samuelson believes the reason for this phenomenon is that America is at a crossroads. He describes the post–World War II period as an "Age of Entitlement"—a heady, optimistic era in which both genuine economic progress and an overpromising government created in many Americans the conviction that a life of unlimited abundance was their birthright. The formula proved irresistible: Earn more money for less work and be completely protected from life's calamities.

Considering the tremendous strides society has made in this century, it's easy to understand why Americans have allowed their expectations to soar. During the 1950s, median family income grew nearly 39 percent over that of the prior decade, even after being adjusted for inflation. In the 1960s, incomes grew another 37 percent on top of that.

Yet, all the while, government was growing too—its budgets and debt exceeded only by its promises.

"In 1929, government spending accounted for about 11 percent of the nation's economic output," Samuelson tells us. "Three percent for the federal government, the rest for states, counties, and municipalities. By 1990, this share had risen to about 38 percent, nearly two-thirds of it federal."

Not surprisingly, the engines propelling this great American entitlement machine are quickly running out of gas. Beginning in the 1970s, government began to rack up huge deficits. The pace of economic growth slackened significantly. Median family income rose just 6 percent in the 1970s and 6 percent in the 1980s—and we've been treading water in the 1990s.

No More Guarantees

Do you risk becoming an "economic ghost"? That's what the *Wall Street Journal* calls the approximately one million men between the ages of 25 and 55 who have simply dropped out of the American workforce. They are generally healthy, and they are not in prison, but for a variety of reasons, they are out of work and no longer actively seek it.

Many, like an unemployed executive in West Hartford, Connecticut, are simply too discouraged to continue a frustrating search to capture a job and recapture a lost lifestyle. "It's an employers' market," the 49-year-old former purchasing agent told the *Journal.* "I'd probably be the last one on the list they would hire." This man, a victim of corporate downsizing, tries to make ends meet with $250 a month in welfare payments.

We have not seen the end of the restructuring underway in the American economy. *USA Today* reported recently that major corporations have laid off more than three million employees since 1989. Sixty percent of the companies regularly surveyed by the American Management Association plan to cut jobs further—the highest percentage in history.

A quiet desperation has settled in across the American landscape—a desperation that is keenly felt by people who on paper are doing well but whose lives are beset by fear and anxiety. The cruelest irony is that the very sense of security for which so many people have subjugated their dreams and wrapped themselves in the protective cloak of government or big business has crumbled away.

When *USA Today* asked baby boomers between the ages of 32 and 50 to write to the newspaper about the experiences and fears of losing their white-collar professional jobs, the responses included poignant and bitter tales of lost self-respect, broken marriages, and even suicide. One reader reported that the ensuing anxiety had poisoned his entire suburban community:

> A bunker mentality has replaced neighborhood fellowship. A nomadic existence has usurped the concept of roots, of living in one place for a lifetime. The security that comes from stability is what baby boomers want most. And it is the very thing that today seems so hard to possess.

Americans are not alone. In Japan, for example, the 1990s have seen the gradual but steady disintegration of the promise of lifetime employment with a single company. "The traditional Japanese system that bound loyal workers and paternalistic employers to each other, in good times and bad, produced a level of commitment and a lack of labor unrest that were unknown in the West," the *New York Times* reported recently. All that's gone now. The harsh new reality is that "the guarantee of a lifelong job . . . is finally beginning to break down."

The High Cost of a Good Life

For every American who fears losing his or her job, there are probably many more who wonder why it now takes two incomes to secure the quality of life formerly provided by one. Sixty percent of women now work outside of the home, which is a startling turnaround from the

1950s. And even the paychecks of two wage earners won't buy key components of the American dream, which is fading out of reach for many families.

It's going to cost at least $123,000 to put a child born this year through four years at a public university when he or she reaches college age. The average new car costs $20,000. Home prices have soared 72 percent over the last decade. Medical costs continue to rise much faster than the rate of inflation. Child care, private-school tuition, and—yes—taxes will take an ever-increasing bite out of hard-earned paychecks. By one estimate, in 10 years you'll have to earn a salary 80 percent higher than the salary you earn today just to keep pace with inflation.

And when both spouses get home from their collective 80 hours of weekly employment, the housework still needs to be done, as does the laundry, the lawn, and all the chores and responsibilities of raising children. This burden has put a strain on many marriages. Home life today is marked by increasing levels of domestic violence, juvenile crime, and drug use by children. It's a trap ensnaring greater numbers of citizens in countries throughout the world.

Unfortunately, growing older will not bring relief. How would you like to live on $1,248 a month? If you retire at age 65 with no other source of income and no savings, that's the *maximum* payment you can get from Social Security. For many Americans, it's a fraction of the income and the lifestyle to which they've grown accustomed.

That fact alone could significantly delay retirement for many in the baby boomer generation. "They won't be able to retire at 55, or maybe even at 65," the *Wall Street Journal* recently reported, "because of inadequate savings, reduced employer benefits, and the likely scaling back of what the federal government will provide."

Maximum Social Security retirement benefits are already scheduled to be pushed back over time to age 67 instead of 65. Ever greater portions of those benefits are likely to be taxed. The benefits themselves are in question. Economist Paul Craig Roberts spells it out bluntly. "The two government programs underwriting an aging population—Medicare and Social Security—are both in financial trouble," he wrote in *Business Week* recently. "According to the 1995 Social Security Trustees Report, retirees face—unless there are substantial increases in the payroll tax—a 10 percent reduction in hospitalization and retirement benefits by the year 2010, a 27 percent reduction by 2020, and a 41 percent reduction by 2040."

Retirement should be a time of serenity, with opportunities to travel, spend time with grandchildren, and do the things you always wanted to do. Increasingly, both government and employers are incapable of providing security or opportunities for older Americans.

THE NEW OPPORTUNITIES

Despite all the bleak forecasts, however, we can also view this present situation positively as a time for change and new opportunities for everyone. Former President Ronald Reagan liked to tell the story about the farm boy who was happily and energetically cleaning out the manure in the stable. When asked why he was approaching his task with such enthusiasm, he replied, "I do it because I just know there's got to be a pony in here somewhere!"

As difficult as employment dislocations are, there is a pony here too. Corporate downsizing has opened up unprecedented opportunities for independent business-people. Our economy has become more entrepreneurial. Leaner corporations are farming out many activities to small firms that can perform the tasks more efficiently than big corporate behemoths can.

Keep in mind that while the American economy has eliminated a total of 43 million jobs in all fields since 1979, it has also created 70 million new jobs—a net increase of 27 million. That's a lot of ponies!

Most of this growth has occurred in the small business sector. "Small business is on a roll," writes Richard Lesher, president of the U.S. Chamber of Commerce in his new book, *Meltdown on Main Street.* "It is without question the most dynamic sector of the economy, creating the bulk of new jobs."

Increasingly, downsized employees as well as voluntary exiles from the corporate jungle are starting their own businesses. According to the *Los Angeles Times,* the number of self-employed Americans now totals anywhere from 12 to 17 percent of the workforce.

* * *

As economic realities have shifted, so has the profile of the people in Amway. The business has always drawn its participants from a wide cross section of occupations. Joe Logan likes to tell the story about sponsoring his dentist in Scottsdale, Arizona, who in turn went out and sponsored a physician, a podiatrist, a paper-mill worker, and a plumber!

There has always been the perception—not entirely without merit—that Amway has drawn most heavily from the ranks of Americans with lower incomes and less education who dwelled principally on farms and in small towns. Amway was seen by many as a last refuge for people who had failed and not as a higher plane of opportunity for those who had already succeeded.

That perception is changing fast. Diamond Direct Distributor Mike Wilson of California puts it bluntly: "It's not a requirement to have hated your life to be in the Amway business."

Executive Diamond Jim Head has seen a marked change in the kind of people who are today joining the Amway business. "I am seeing very wealthy and successful people, top-quality people—from Coeur d'Alene, Idaho, to Lake Tahoe to Newport Beach—get really excited about the business," he told me. "They're starting from zero like everyone else and they don't care. Business is booming!"

Jim is bemused by his observation because he recalls that when he and his wife, Judy, got into the business in the early 1980s, they were told that the market was already saturated. There was no more room for Amway to grow. It just goes to show you that the conventional wisdom is always conventional and almost always wrong!

Maybe it was Jim's unconventional background as a rock musician in the Southern California music scene that prompted him to turn a deaf ear to the naysayers. Today, Jim and Judy divide their time between homes in Idaho, Las Vegas, and Lake Arrowhead, California. As they continue to build their business, the Heads get great satisfaction from helping bring to others what Amway has brought to them—the opportunity to take responsibility for their own lives and set themselves free.

Materialism and Idealism

From Harvard to Amway? A few years ago, people might have said, "No way!" But both Ian and Nancy Gamson have degrees from Harvard and a successful Amway business at the Diamond level. (This high brainpower match came about because Nancy fell in love with Ian's Australian accent!)

Ian spent much of his boyhood on Fiji, where his father worked for a big sugar company. His early schooling took place in a two-room schoolhouse. After attending boarding school back in Australia (where he remembers well the sting of the headmaster's corporal punishment), he earned a B.A. from the University of Sydney and was accepted in a graduate program that took him to Harvard. He met Nancy there in a philosophy class.

When they completed their studies, Ian went back to Australia, while Nancy returned home to Minnesota. The couple became engaged through the mailbox. After they married and spent some time traveling, the couple settled in Minnesota while Ian pursued a Ph.D. in history.

The accumulation of academic degrees, however, failed to establish a clear direction for the Gamsons. They developed what we would call in today's parlance a great deal of "attitude" about business and the need to make money. In fact, they were pretty good at *not* making money. By the time Ian got his Ph.D., they were still living with Nancy's mother, they had three children, and they were $55,000 in debt. "We were in a bitter midlife crisis," Nancy recalls. Even so, their intellectual idealism—some would say pride—stood in the way of escaping to something better.

The first time they were told about Amway, Nancy was skeptical. But Ian had been convinced, and he had to practically drag Nancy back to additional meetings.

"Don't give up on the people who resist the struggle between materialism and idealism," Nancy now advises. What turned things around for her was when her oldest son needed a $1,500 operation to repair a deformity in his jaw for which he was being ridiculed by other children at school. They couldn't afford the operation and had to borrow the money. It changed the little boy's life.

Today, both Ian and Nancy Gamson understand and attempt to convey to others that it's not materialism but rather the height of idealism "when you make other people's dreams come true."

Nancy directs a special message to professional women. "Many women achieve success in the Amway business," she asserts. "Why must we choose between career and children? I want it all!"

Prescription for Success

Cliff and Kathy Minter of California thought they would have it all when Cliff achieved his dream of a career in medicine, an honored and lucrative profession. "I loved my profession. I enjoyed it. As a podiatrist, I was involved in sports medicine, and it was an exciting career."

Cliff woke up one day when he saw, strangely enough, other doctors walking away from their practices for a business called Amway. For them, the medical profession was simply not delivering as promised. HMOs turned many doctors into corporate employees. Malpractice suits made them targets for economic ruin. The dream of helping people seemed to fade into the sunset.

"Recognition, a sense of belonging, security, cash flow, and freedom—many doctors and other highly skilled people used to get these things in their occupations. Now they find them in Amway," Cliff told me. "I can help more people in a greater way than I could as a doctor. There has never been a better way to help people. And this business has helped *me* grow as a person. I've become a better father and husband because of it.

"I know a lot of people, including many in the medical profession, who, if asked whether they would want their son or daughter to live the same life they are leading, would say no. But go ask Amway Diamonds whether the lives they are leading are good enough for their children, and they'll say yes!"

Today, Cliff and Kathy Minter are Executive Diamonds, and for Cliff, building the business is his passion: "For me, it doesn't even seem like work."

Doing Something Right the First Time

Pat and Betty Kaufmann both liked their jobs, too. He was a metallurgist and she a medical technologist. When a friend of Pat's first showed them the Amway business plan, "on a scale of one to a hundred, we were a zero," he remembers. It's not that they didn't have very strong and ambitious goals: "We had vowed to become millionaires by age 40." The Kaufmanns were always looking for ways to get ahead, but as highly skilled professionals, they looked down on selling. It seemed beneath them.

A few more meetings gradually turned Pat's attitude around. Betty came around more slowly. They worked for two years to become Direct Distributors. By the end of the next two years, they had duplicated in their Amway business the entire combined income of both paychecks. "We reached the point where our entire paychecks from our salaried jobs were going into investments and savings," Pat marvels.

The Kaufmanns' business took off when they no longer allowed a condescending attitude about sales get in the way of their intelligence. The logic behind Amway was simply too clear and too strong. "The power driving this business is the idea of ongoing income," Pat told me. "You do something right one time, and it can pay you for a long time. I don't know of anything else anywhere that offers that."

Betty says, "A lot of people in very high-level professions are working more and more hours and getting less money to do it. There's a new group of medical professionals in California, for example, who are all joining the business. You now have the Amway Plan being shown in the living rooms of multimillion-dollar homes."

Today, Pat and Betty Kaufmann are at Amway's Executive Diamond level, and they help lead one of the business's largest organizations of distributors, International Connection. They run an international business from their home in Bend, Oregon—a business that stretches from Asia to South America to Europe. When Amway opened its doors in Colombia on August 1, 1996, the Kaufmanns' organization signed up hundreds of new distributors on the first day.

Breaking Free from Poverty of the Soul

Amway is a business that can appeal equally to the person struggling to rise out of abject poverty as well as to the person who has made it to the top of a highly skilled profession only to find that the profession has changed. Doctors, lawyers, teachers, corporate executives, and many others are finding that the dreams and values that led them to their professions now have a more welcome home in Amway.

Amway provides an unsurpassed opportunity for millions of people in the United States and around the world to make the personal transition from a life of dependency and doubt to one of independence and self-sufficiency.

There's a common spirit that is really catching fire among people of vastly different circumstances, nationalities, backgrounds, races, religions, and ethnicity. People are talking about Amway—from the sidewalks of Bogotá, Colombia, to the living rooms of those multimillion-dollar homes in Orange County, California.

Why? Because people are dreaming of a better life, but they see no clear path for getting there.

They don't like dangling at the end of strings held by corporate decision makers, but they're afraid to cut the strings themselves. "What about my salary path? What about my benefits? What will people think of me?" they wonder.

These people may want more than anything to provide their kids with a better education than they had. They know education really begins in the home; the only problem is, they're never home to offer that guidance. They fear for what could happen to their children after school—in the neighborhood or on the playground.

They want the freedom to retire at an age when they're still healthy enough to enjoy new adventures. But they also want the freedom *not* to retire, to continue to do useful and profitable things and not to feel they're going to be pushed out the door after years of service.

They can't really depend on the government to take care of them when they are old and sick. More important, they don't *want* to depend on government assistance. They want to do for themselves.

As I meet those who have found success in Amway, I see people breaking free from poverty—poverty of the pocketbook and poverty of the soul.

"It's crazy to have to work 40 or 50 years and then have nothing to show for it," Diamond Direct Distributor Frank Morales told me. "What amazes me is how many people don't even sit down for one single hour to plan for their future. They're just sitting there waiting for things to happen instead of taking charge."

The Only Sure Thing in This Economy

Jim Floor was a high-powered lobbyist in Sacramento, California—a successful person. But it meant long hours away from home, and Jim saw a kind of irony in the fact that the higher up people rose in his corporation—or in any corporation—the less time and independence they had. "Wasn't it supposed to be the other way around?" he wondered. "They wanted you to marry the corporate structure," Jim says, recalling that it was Margee he chose to marry, not a company.

So the Floors started an Amway business in 1979, seeking to establish a cash flow that would one day enable Jim to leave his job. "You can begin to create that cash flow while still working in your present career. That's the beauty of it," Jim told me. "Once you succeed, then it becomes a question of how you want to spend your day.

"This business offers what so many people are missing today in their lives—an opportunity to be in business for yourself with total control over your own life. I was in the corporate structure for 16 years, so I know how you cave in, how you give in. Then you stop and look at your life and you ask yourself, 'How did I get to this?'"

Jim Floor also reflected on the sense of isolation people can experience in the business world. "Whether you're in a corporation or even running your own company, it's often a very lonely road and very competitive. What seems unique about Amway is that it offers you the opportunity to build long-term business relationships, which lead to long-term personal relationships.

"As I look back on my experience in the business, the number one benefit is the personal growth. That's what really adds to your quality of life. If Amway closed its doors tomorrow, if everything else just suddenly disappeared, that's the one thing no one could take away."

Today, Jim and Margee Floor work full time and together in their Amway business, at the Executive Diamond level. In their view, the business fits the times we live in perfectly. "Margee and I want people to experience what we have experienced—we've reached our financial goals," Jim says. "For the 17 years we have been in Amway, both the business itself and our income have gotten better and better, while the average person's job has become less secure and his income has decreased— or maybe changed insignificantly. This business is the only sure thing in this economy."

Will you belong to the best of times or will you belong to the worst of times? The choice rests only with you. So does the responsibility to *make* that choice.

3

Business in a Box

"I was out with a friend who was starting his second year of law school," Executive Diamond Ray Melillo recalls. "We were sitting in my car at midnight, and he started talking about this business opportunity. He said he wished he'd seen this business opportunity before starting law school. Then he started drawing the Amway Sales and Marketing Plan on the back of an envelope."

Several years later, Ray's future wife, Joanne, was commuting on a train to her job at a New York law firm. "A young woman was excitedly talking about this business opportunity she'd seen. I pressed her for information about it, but she wouldn't share anything with me. . . . But after 30 minutes of prying, I finally persuaded her to give me a phone number."

That phone number led Joanne to a presentation of the Plan. It was there she met Ray. It was there she was introduced to Amway. Ray and Joanne married and built their highly successful Amway business together.

It's officially called the Amway Sales and Marketing Plan, but Amway distributors—from newcomers to old-timers—invariably call it the Plan. For many, the first time the Plan was presented to them stands out as a momentous event in their lives. They vividly recall the time, place, circumstances, and their initial reaction the way the rest of us recall meeting spouses, launching a new career, or learning of an epochal event in history.

To comprehend the powerful response the Amway Plan has evoked and to evaluate it fairly alongside other business opportunities—and perhaps, to peel away some inaccurate stereotypes you may be harboring—there are a few things readers who are not part of Amway need to understand. First, on a practical level, the Plan sets forth the methods, formulas, and levels of achievement according to which the Amway distributor earns both income and recognition.

Who is eligible to be an Amway distributor? Everyone who passes the age test! You must be 16 years old to be a distributor and 18 years of age to sponsor others. To become a Direct Distributor (an important milestone, which I'll explain shortly), you must attain the age that your state considers adulthood. There are no other requirements, other than fulfilling your promise to abide by the Amway Rules of Conduct and Code of Ethics (see the appendix).

When you become an Amway distributor, you do *not* become an Amway employee. The flip side of that coin is that *you*, not Amway, own your business. It becomes a potentially valuable family asset. Your of-age children can help you build it, and you may bequeath your distributorship to your heirs when you die.

THE PLAN

In the Amway Plan, two tasks are identified as front and center as you build your business: creating a small core of repeat customers and then duplicating your efforts by enlisting others to do the same.

You start by personally using a rapidly growing and internationally respected line of high-quality products (and in some countries, services). Using your own products only makes sense—you should be your own best customer, especially when you enjoy a discount on all the products. The fact is that product knowledge and enthusiasm flow out of using and liking the products.

Since many products can reach your customers directly from the company's own warehouses, selling the product has never been easier. Many Amway distributors also find that some people do not sign up to become distributors but are nevertheless attracted to the product line and become good repeat customers. So don't fear that selling products is "the little giant killer" that might stop you from grabbing on to this opportunity. Just start creating your team of distributors, and the products will help bring you customers.

Because the Plan has different features and benefits (as well as product lines) in different countries, I will refrain from describing it in further detail. But, clearly, the path to greater success and profitability depends on your ability to sponsor other distributors, who comprise what is commonly known as your downline. You *don't* make money simply by signing distributors up—you *do* make money when they actually sell the products themselves. You keep on earning as long as they keep on generating volume (and so long as you abide by the rules of conduct).

You'll hear Amway distributors talk frequently about the two different scales that are used to calculate business activities. The first is Business Volume (BV), which is an assigned number for each product you sell. Each product is also assigned a Point Value (PV), which is normally about 50 percent of the product's BV dollar amount. Both scales are used to calculate the various bonuses that Amway or upline distributors pay as well as to determine the level of success a distributor has achieved under the Plan.

Once you reach a combined PV of 7,500 a month in sales and maintain it for six months within the Amway fiscal year (three months must be consecutive), you become a Direct Distributor. (These numbers apply to North America only. The Plan is modified to fit the different laws and realities of each country in which Amway operates.)

At the Direct Distributor level, you break off from your sponsoring distributor (although he or she continues to derive income from your sales, paid by the Amway Corporation) and you receive your Performance Bonus directly from Amway. Once you become a Direct Distributor, you are eligible for a whole new menu of additional incentives, awards, expense-paid trips, and recognition.

Although there are several exciting levels along the way, most Direct Distributors set their sights on achieving the Diamond level—"Diamond is where it's at" is a common saying among Amway leaders. The Diamond level is achieved when a Direct Distributor helps six different groups achieve the 7,500 Point Value for six months of each fiscal year (three months must be consecutive for first-time qualifiers).

How much income does a Diamond make? In 1982, in his book *An Uncommon Freedom*, Charles Paul Conn pegged the income at around $75,000; taking inflation into account as well as several enhancements to the Plan since that time, we can deduce that this figure is substantially higher today. From the Diamond level, you can reach the Executive Diamond, Double Diamond, Triple Diamond, Crown, and Crown Ambassador levels. Among Amway leaders there is talk that as a result of the spectacular success of distributors like Peter and Eva Mueller-Meerkatz of Germany, the company is contemplating the creation of a new level beyond Crown Ambassador.

The Plan. It's an inventive blend of incentives designed to bring out the best in people, ignite their entrepreneurial spirit, and reward hard work with a steadily escalating array of financial rewards and—just as important—*recognition.*

What the Plan does *not* do is promise something for nothing. It does *not* suggest you'll get rich quick or even get rich at all. The Plan offers you a low-cost business opportunity and a powerful set of reasons to perform. And, contrary to the "dog eat dog" reputation that capitalism has earned in some quarters, Amway's Plan rewards you for helping others prosper. Your success is determined not by how many competitors you beat down but by how many people you help succeed.

Amway's Ladder of Achievement

Reaching higher steps on the Amway ladder brings increasingly greater recognition and financial rewards, including expense-paid trips to resorts; seminars and conferences on one of Amway's luxurious *Enterprise* motor yachts; large lump sum bonuses; profile articles in the *Amagram*, the company's monthly magazine; and prominent speaking and training roles at motivational conferences.

One thing Amway people will tell you: it's never too late—nor is it ever too soon—to start climbing that ladder!

Rod and Rowena Jao of British Columbia are just 22 years old and have already achieved Diamond status. Rod, the son of Filipino immigrants, never doubted he would be successful in his own business. By age 19, he had reached Amway's Ruby level and was spending so much time building his business that Rowena decided the only way she would ever get to see Rod was to join him and do it as a team.

THE PRODUCTS

Although Amway is still frequently derided as a "soap-suds" company or misunderstood as a firm specializing in generic, "no-name" brands, over the years it has developed an extraordinary offering of more than 6,500 high-quality products and services.

Amway's Core-Line Products today include more than 400 personal-care and home-tech products that carry the Amway brand name. Many of these are developed, tested, manufactured, packaged, and shipped out of Amway's state-of-the-art facilities at its Ada, Michigan, headquarters. The wide-ranging line of products includes:

- Personal-care, home-care, and car-care products, including such popular staples as L.O.C. (Liquid

Organic Cleaner) Multi-Purpose Cleaner and SA8 Laundry Concentrate
* Artistry cosmetics and skin-care products
* Nutrilite vitamins and food supplements and a side variety of other food products, including the Shaq Bar, a high-energy food bar named for basketball great Shaquille O'Neal
* The Amway Water Treatment System, which in 1995 sold more than 450,000 units throughout North America, Japan, and the Asia-Pacific region

Suggested retail prices for Amway products are very competitive, especially considering the service and convenience the customer receives by having products delivered right to his or her home. For the distributor, they're a high-quality bargain. Distributors purchase the products for sale to customers or for their own use at wholesale prices that are generally 30 percent below suggested retail prices. All products are backed by a money-back guarantee.

Amway's Catalog Products represent the company's effort to tap into an ongoing revolution in the way we buy things—and it is substantially reshaping the company's image and appeal for consumers and distributors alike.

"The network-marketing industry is rapidly evolving into a gigantic distribution freeway," writes Richard Poe in *Wave 3: The New Era in Network Marketing* (Prima). "In the future, network-marketing companies will serve more as distribution freeways than as a specialized sales force for a single manufacturer. Astute investors will take note of the rapidly formed virtual alliances that take place along that freeway."

The future Poe envisions is the here and now for Amway. The company has teamed up with hundreds of product manufacturing and service companies to offer thousands of brand-name products, which distributors can pitch to customers, who then can call or fax in their orders to Amway.

A soap company indeed! Leaf through the Personal Shoppers Catalog and find a vast array of name-brand products from Pierre Cardin to Hershey's. Amway Services are offered as well. Major service joint ventures include MCI long-distance calling (Amway was a significant force in helping MCI emerge as a major competitor to AT&T), a VISA credit card, Northwest Airlines travel, and AMVOX Network Voice Messaging, an electronic voice mail service.

Why do so many famous names in manufacturing now want to be included in Amway's product offerings? It's the immediate access to a highly motivated sales force operating in more than 70 countries and territories around the world. For the distributor, it puts him or her in the driver's seat on that ever-changing and expanding distribution highway.

THE PHILOSOPHY

Which would you rather have? A million bucks cash right now, or one cent with a guarantee that it will double in value every day for a month?

If you take the million dollars, you're a sucker. You just threw away a $4.2 million fortune in a 30-day month and $8.4 million in a 31-day month. If you don't believe me, there's a blank page opposite the back cover of this book where you can figure it out!

Amway prefers to call itself a *direct-selling* company, meaning that it bypasses one or more movements in the product distribution chain. The most obviously eliminated step is the retail outlet. Instead of the scenario of a manufacturing company sending products to one or more distributors and wholesalers who in turn deliver the products to the stores, you have the direct-selling scenario, in which products are sold directly to the consumer by a distributor who acquires his or her inventory straight from the manufacturer. Distributors are paid according to the volume and the value of products they move.

Amway can also be called a *network-marketing* organization because distributors rely heavily on personal contacts—their network of friends, associates, and friends of friends and associates—for selling products, rather than the more traditional marketing methods, such as mass media advertising.

And it can be called a *multilevel-marketing* business, since distributors make money not only by selling products but by convincing others to do the same. Upline and downline business relationships continue to determine the distribution of ongoing business income. You will often hear Amway distributors identify themselves by saying, for example, "I'm in the Miller Diamond organization, which is part of Britt Worldwide." They are referring to their various upline distributors—a kind of Amway family tree.

As for another term frequently thrown around in this arena of business activity—"pyramid"—Amway has put such accusations to rest from both legal and business standpoints: the FTC ruled in 1979 that Amway was not a pyramid but a legitimate business. (See chapter 10 for a more technical discussion of this subject.)

AMWAY AND THE CONSUMER REVOLUTION

Amway is thriving today because it has positioned itself in the forefront of a consumer revolution that emphasizes convenience, quality, and personal service.

Can you remember the following times?

- You had to do all your banking between the hours of 9 A.M. and 2 P.M., Monday through Friday. If you forgot to get cash from the bank by Friday afternoon, you were out of luck until Monday.
- There was no place to buy milk, bread, or aspirin after 9 P.M. at night.
- It was "cash only" at the grocery store. No checks. No credit cards.
- The phone company—not you—owned the phone instruments in your home and offered them in two or three styles and colors. An installer came to your house to put them in, and once they did, you couldn't move them around—no plug-in jacks.

I can remember every one of the "thens" in these "that was then, this is now" scenarios. I suspect you could come up with a list of your own "gee whiz!" changes.

Today, I buy my products from catalogs, book my travel on the Internet, shop 24 hours a day, and never worry about cash being on hand because there's always an ATM close by, even when I'm thousands of miles away from my hometown bank.

Convenience and quality are the orders of the day—sometimes even outranking price as factors. As consumers, we're busier than ever, yet we have more choices than ever before, particularly with the dramatic increase in our access to information and technology. Worldwide demand for a vast array of new products, along with heightened global competition, compels companies to change their ways, too.

Some of the changes that we consider new and revolutionary are in fact modern derivations of the tried and true. Rural, small-town America has a long history of reliance on door-to-door selling and mail-order shopping. Farm families and others who were located far from sizable towns and cities simply had no other choice.

Amway thus represents a return to a more personal, neighbor-to-neighbor approach to commerce and, at the same time, an eager embrace of the new ways in which goods and services are made, shipped, sold, and bought. It is a highly personal business in an era of high technology. Amway is successful today because it hasn't forgotten or forsaken the role of people in the equation of global commerce.

SUCCEEDING WITHOUT EXPERIENCE OR CAPITAL

Most people are poorly prepared for entrepreneurship—even those who have climbed to high ranks in the corporate world's best companies.

I should know. I'm one of them. Like many white-collar professionals, I accumulated a lot of experience in the *boardrooms* of business but no experience in the *back rooms* of business. Maybe you find yourself in this same boat:

- You've never met a payroll and never kept a set of books.
- You've never negotiated for office space, leased equipment, or contracted for services.
- You've never applied for business licenses, paid fees, or secured health insurance for employees.
- You've never lugged sample cases and displays through airports and customs.
- You've never hired a lawyer to approve contracts or collect unpaid debts from deadbeats.

Rex Renfrow worked for the federal government in Washington, D.C., climbing from lowly beginnings as a GS-3 clerk typist to GS-14. A government job: the ultimate in cradle-to-grave security. But it wasn't enough.

"I had a dream to own my own business," Rex recalls. "But after spending half a lifetime trying, I began to think the dream could not come true. The crowning blow fell when my superiors told me that someone like me without a college degree could advance no further no matter how hard I worked or how well I did my job."

No special talent. No special knowledge. No family business at which to apprentice and one day inherit. Rex Renfrow was one of millions who dream of owning their own business but don't have the tools to build the dream into reality. It was not until Rex heard about Amway and joined the business that he was able to find a path to success.

While many lack the knowledge to start a successful business, others lack the capital. Even small businesses can cost big money to start. According to *Entrepreneur* magazine, typical start-up fees for franchises can range anywhere from a low end of $3,000 for a shopping bag advertising company to a midrange of $60,000 for an antique and custom furniture franchise to a high end of $200,000 and up for long-distance reselling services or fancy car wash businesses.

Still others are handicapped by a lack of discipline or are paralyzed by the fear of rejection. It's not easy to start a business today. Most small businesses fail.

Many now-successful Amway distributors learned these lessons, the hard way, pouring their energies and life savings into other kinds of businesses that didn't work out. Triple Diamond Tim Foley describes his expensive odyssey as he attempted to establish his financial life before his professional football career ended: "During those 11 seasons in Miami, I invested in real estate and lost some money. I invested in the stock market and lost some money. I invested in gold and precious metals and lost money there as well. Finally, I invested in health clubs and racquetball courts, and though the business prospered for a while, interest rates rose to 21 percent and new memberships slowed, then finally trickled to a stop."

Cecilia Karasz, a Diamond Direct Distributor from Hungary, tried to get numerous businesses off the ground before the Amway opportunity presented itself.

From today's position of success she can now joke about all the false starts: "Some people collect stamps; I collected businesses."

Others found success in business but lost a sense of balance in their lives. Bob and Jackie Zeender of Silver Spring, Maryland, were among them. They owned a successful and acclaimed restaurant, which brought not only a good income but recognition and respect from peers—as evidenced by Bob's election as president of the Washington Restaurant Association.

Why would a couple achieving both financial security and recognition in their own business even give Amway a second look? The never-ending daily grind of running a restaurant was the reason; they worked long hours and had an exhausting schedule that was punctuated by scarce, fleeting moments with their two children.

Today, Bob and Jackie Zeender own a successful Amway business that allows them to set a flexible work schedule, be full-time parents, and contribute to society through their work in charity. For the Zeenders and many others, Amway has proven to be a business with balance.

* * *

A lot of unlikely things happen in the Amway business, and how Brian Hays got started in Amway is one of them. Brian Hays knows the world of business inside and out; by the age of 27, he was a top executive at Motorola. He is in a unique position to know and to compare businesses. Six weeks after being transferred to a new, higher post in Illinois, a truck driver approached him and introduced him to Amway. Brian wasn't that interested, but his wife, Marguerite, was, and she got the business started. It was Marguerite's success that caught Brian's full attention. "I might be slow, but I'm not stupid," he told me, poking fun at himself.

Within three years, Brian was able to leave Motorola—and he had yet to turn 30 years old! The Hayses have been working full time in their Amway business for 26 years now, building it to the Triple Diamond level and helping lead one of Amway's successful distributor support organizations, International Connection.

"I was one of the very early professionals to get into the business," Brian told me. "The big thing for other professionals to know is that you can easily build this business around your career and make the break if and when you are ready."

An insatiable entrepreneur, Brian Hays dabbled in other ventures along the way. "I got stupid and got involved in businesses that required a lot of capital, overhead, and employees, and all the headaches that come with them," he says. "Our Amway business requires so little overhead that we are running a worldwide business out of our home with the help of a part-time secretary. There are no territories. There are no boundaries."

THE KIT

Brian Hays would tell us that there are literally thousands of business opportunities available in this age of entrepreneurship. Some are better than others; many are good opportunities. But I haven't found any that come close to Amway in terms of its accessibility, affordability, and flexibility.

It costs only about $135 to start a business that could change your life. That's the price for the Amway Business Kit, a package of products and materials designed for the new distributor. Helpful as it is, the Amway Business Kit is not all there is to building a successful business, but it's a vivid illustration of the openness of this business to all. No one is guaranteed success, but everyone is guaranteed a chance—no matter how low your income, no matter how scarce your capital, no matter how limited your level of education. Whether you've tried other businesses and failed, tried them and succeeded, or never tried them at all, you will be surprised at how simple it is to begin this business with your sponsor and upline to teach you and help you succeed. There's nothing else like it on the market today.

One thing they can't put in the Business Kit is the people of Amway. Striking out on your own takes courage. No one wants to be all alone in a leaky rowboat bobbing around in the middle of a stormy sea. But when you team up with a solid and reputable organization like Amway as well as one of the major distributor organizations, then you are not alone or at a disadvantage:

- You will be guided by your sponsor and upline distributors, who have every interest in your success. When you win, they win. It's that simple.
- You will have the strong advantage of quality products, with the good name of Amway backing them up.
- You will have a tradition of innovation that will ensure you are in a leading-edge business that is

continually developing new products, embarking on new joint ventures, and exploring new markets.

- Amway's "business in a box" approach equips you with effective tools to make your transition from dependence to independence as mistake-free as possible.

In this business, the number one asset is people. You might be surprised how many assets you can bring to the table. It has been estimated that the typical American adult over the age of 25 knows some 2,000 people by their first names.

Chances are, you've already got a potential network of distributors and don't even know it!

4

A Family Affair

They were seated in the boat, Nick in the stern, his father rowing. The sun was coming up over the hills. A bass jumped, making a circle in the water. Nick trailed his hand in the water. It felt warm in the sharp chill of the morning.

In the early morning on the lake in the stern of the boat with his father rowing, he felt quite sure he would never die.
—Ernest Hemingway, "Indian Camp"

In the lobby of the Amway World Headquarters in Ada, Michigan, hangs a mural that is 7 feet high and 20 feet long. It's called "The Bond." Presented to Jay Van Andel and Rich DeVos in 1985 by artist Paul Collins, the painting weaves together a series of vignettes that tell the Amway story: the hard road to success, the country that made it possible, the legendary distributors who to this day propel Amway to new levels of achievement. All are bonded together—the people, the values, the country, the history—to tell this remarkable story.

What stands out more than anything else in "The Bond" is the role of family in the lives of the cofounders and in the milestones they have achieved. The center-piece of the mural is a portrait of Jay, flanked on one side by his wife, Betty, and their four children; next to Jay is Rich, flanked on the other side by his wife, Helen, and *their* four children.

Family stands at the center of the Amway miracle— not just for the founders but for Amway distributors both famous and unknown around the world. Virtually every person I have heard from in this business has praised Amway for the role it has played in strengthening or even saving their families.

It is a business that families can build together and pass on to future generations. It is a business that can be built without putting the family's financial foundation in jeopardy: one spouse can initially take the lead, while the other continues to draw a steady paycheck from a salaried position. It is a business that has prevented divorce and prompted touching reconciliations of parents and children after decades of estrangement. It is a business that serves as a loving family for those who have none.

What a stark contrast to the state of the family in our society at large! Thirty percent of all American children are now born out of wedlock—nearly 25 percent of white Americans and 70 percent of African Americans. In two-parent families, both spouses working outside the home has become the rule and not the exception. Commutes are longer, demands on the job are greater; children and spouses increasingly take a back seat to the career. Many families have become strangers, their lives intersecting only in the early morning or late at night.

Meanwhile, an overburdened Social Security system and the ever-increasing taxes needed to support it are causing conflicts among the generations. Elders are often seen as a burden rather than a precious resource. The American family is facing a crisis; Amway families have found solutions.

STRENGTHENING THE BOND

Craig Holiday had always dreamed of being the dad he never knew. His father had left his family when Craig was seven years old. His mother had suffered from a serious drinking problem, and the boy was often left in the care of relatives. History almost repeated itself.

But his dream was shattered in the late 1970s, when he returned home after another bout of late-night drinking with his buddies. He found a note on the kitchen table from his wife, Carole, which said, "I've decided to leave you. Until you change your life, I won't come back."

As devastated as he was, Craig knew it was coming. He was lost and aimless. The construction company he owned didn't satisfy him. His real estate deals went bad. Ashamed of failure, he pulled away from Carole, spending his nights drinking with his friends instead. "I didn't even know my friends' wives' names," he remembers sadly, "because they called them their 'old lady.'"

"We were broke and broken," Carole says of their lives back then. "It was an emotional bankruptcy. We couldn't pay our bills. We were $250,000 in debt. All I could do was pray that my husband's self-esteem would be restored."

The Holidays sold their furniture to pay bills. Soon, they were living in an empty house—empty of possessions and empty of hope. "We would have gotten divorced," Carole said, "but we couldn't afford that either."

Two weeks after Craig found Carole's note, Dan and Jeanette Robinson showed them the Amway Sales and Marketing Plan. At first, Carole wouldn't listen to the tapes; Craig said he didn't have time. But soon, more out of desperation than inspiration, they began to build a business. "We built it fast because we didn't have anything else," Craig said. "We had nothing else. We were just a couple that was devastated and broke. I never dreamed of being in the Amway business, but I always dreamed of being somebody."

More than 15 years later, Executive Diamonds Craig and Carole Holiday reminisce with fondness about all the blessings their business has brought to them. The trips with their friends to the Far East, their shopping sprees in New York City, the fishing trips in Alaska, their beautiful home overlooking the Pacific Ocean. But what matters the most is what the business has done for their lives. "The real victory of this business is the victory within," Carole says. "We learned to love one another again."

She will always treasure a magical night in Thailand, where she and Craig were attending a meeting of successful Amway distributors. "We went to a beautiful place called the Rose Garden, a resort about an hour outside of Bangkok," she remembers. "It was like the Garden of Eden." There were flowers everywhere and little children in traditional costumes carrying candles and baskets of orchids. As the sun set, the Holidays and their group were treated to a fabulous banquet, with Thai dancers entertaining them as they enjoyed the local food. They had come a long way from an empty house and shattered dreams.

"Then Craig asked me to dance," Carole says, "and he gave me flowers. There I was, dancing in the Garden of Eden. This never would have happened if we had not been given the opportunity to turn our lives around. We never would have been a couple."

Just as he had dreamed and promised to himself, Craig set out to be a good full-time dad to his three children. But one demon remained trapped inside—the hatred he felt for his own father who had left when Craig was a boy.

"Finally, I realized the only person in bondage was me, because I was carrying all that hate around with me," Craig explains. "That's when I decided to forgive my father. I invited him to a leadership meeting and invited him up on the stage with me and asked for his forgiveness. By taking this step, I experienced a complete healing from my anger." Today, Craig Holiday oversees Moriah Ministries, an organization he founded for men seeking reconciliation with their fathers.

* * *

Executive Diamond Cliff Minter has thought a lot about the impact of Amway on fathers. Growing up as a battered child, Cliff tried to compensate by being an overachiever, even at the expense of his role as a father and a husband.

"Men are basically wimps," he says. "They're good when they control the environment around them. I'm a podiatrist. Put me in an operating room, and I'm great. But when taken out of the comfort zone, men get insecure and they quit. There's no question I'd be divorced now if it were not for Amway. I know many others in this business who feel the same way."

Much is made of the fact (and with good reason) that the business has allowed many women to choose to stay at home with their children while at the same time earning an income and achieving professional satisfaction. Cliff also reminds us that in a society sorely lacking good male role models, Amway is full of "men who are growing in character and establishing tremendous relationships with their wives and children."

In this last statement, Cliff Minter could have been talking about Larry Koning. Larry is an obstetrician-gynecologist who was once putting in torturous hours at his practice, while Julie, a former nurse, stayed home to raise the couple's two sons.

"Doctors are ripped away from family life by that crazy beeper," says Julie. "Medicine is like another woman. You can easily lose your husband to the profession, and that's what was happening. I saw in this business a way to win my husband back."

The Konings have reached the Diamond level, and Larry has cut his medical practice in half. Both parents are closely involved with their sons' school activities. "That's very unusual," says Julie. "It's usually one parent or another." The Konings attribute their boys' positive attitudes to their exposure to the many successful people in the Amway business.

Brother's Keeper

When I got a call from Brad Duncan, I had to double-check and make sure I knew which Duncan I was talking to! After all, it seems like there are so many successful Duncans in the Amway business, you need a family tree to figure it all out. Brad and Julie Duncan are Double Diamonds. So are Brad's brother Greg and his wife,

Laurie. Another brother is a Direct Distributor. And the brothers' parents are Diamonds!

In Brad's eyes, the family's entrepreneurial drive came from their father. "We were raised in Montana, where my father was successful in all kinds of businesses," he told me. "He did it all on his own, pushing and pushing to get the job done."

Yet as Brad grew into adulthood, he struggled to find a focus. "I was kind of a party guy in school." It showed in his grades and he was kicked out of college.

Meanwhile, in Seattle, older brother Greg had completed nine years of college to become a plastic surgeon. He never opened a practice. Why? Because Greg realized that his Amway business could give him everything he had hoped to realize from medicine—and more. Most important, he didn't want to be married to his practice; he wanted to put family first. Today, while many in the medical profession struggle, Greg and Laurie are millionaires.

And it was Greg who helped his brother Brad find his way. After leaving school, Brad, at age 22, worked in the construction industry for precisely one year. He retired at 23 and hasn't worked for anyone since. That's because Greg showed him the Amway Plan, and Brad and Julie built it with a vengeance. Only in their thirties, they earn a large six-figure income and own three homes. They don't worry about frequent-flyer points because they don't fly commercially; they have their own plane.

Crediting much of their success to the inspiration and guidance of Ron and Georgia Lee Puryear and Bill and Peggy Britt, Brad reflects: "This business teaches us how to listen to people again and start learning again, so that we can start succeeding again."

Remembering What's Important

January 2, 1979, 10:30 A.M.—it's a date and time Executive Diamond Theron Nelsen will never forget. "That's when I saw my last patient, after eight years of practicing optometry."

It also marks the date and time that Theron began devoting himself full time to his and wife Darlene's successful Amway business. "We were looking for the kind of lifestyle this business offered, and we achieved it," Theron says. "So many people today wonder whether their livelihood's going to be with them tomorrow. We don't have to worry about ours not being there."

A medical practice alerted Theron to the kind of life he didn't want to lead. But his experience coaching freshman football taught him valuable lessons about how to succeed in Amway. "In football," he reflects, "you retain your individuality, but you're very much part of a team. And when you coach, you have to bring your players along at different speeds. They respond to different things." A member of the World Wide Dreambuilders organization, Theron's observations from his football days lead him to stress the value of coaching and teamwork in the Amway business.

Yet for the Nelsens, the real test of the business comes down to this—the kind of legacy they will leave to their three children. "Probably 2 percent of parents want their children to follow in their footsteps," Theron says, "and I have not been encouraging mine to go into optometry.

"But you'll always find successful Amway people proudly encouraging their children to follow in their footsteps. It's a business that takes the drift out of the future."

AN EXTENDED FAMILY

Amway has given working women the opportunity and the option to return to the home to care for their children. It has turned part-time fathers into full-time dads. It has brought couples who had been leading separate lives back together to pursue common dreams.

It's also an understanding and forgiving business, enabling families to come together in times of crisis. Crown Ambassadors Jim and Nancy Dornan learned that lesson well.

After graduating from Purdue University, the couple moved to California, where Jim built a career as an aeronautical engineer and Nancy that of a speech pathologist. They quit these jobs when they were 25 years old to pursue, through Amway, their dream of financial independence.

Then the Dornans' second son, Eric, was born with spina bifida. The family was devastated, emotionally and financially. "Eric required 10 to 15 brain surgeries in the space of two years," Jim told me. "We had no family insurance, and we needed options. We were in the Amway business, but we really needed to build it. From 1976 to 1979, we went all the way from Direct Distributors to Crown."

The Dornans' Amway business gave them the freedom to care for Eric and to be there with him during his painful ordeal. "We learned that up to 70 percent of the fathers whose children are born permanently handicapped end up leaving their families because they just can't stand the grief, the guilt, and the financial failure that all too often go with the territory," Jim said. "But with our own business, we not only continue to take care of Eric's expenses, we can reach out to help others who are not as fortunate as we have been."

* * *

Amway's powerful healing impact on the nuclear family is undeniable. Many have also found a kind of extended family in their Amway business partners, caring for one another in good times and bad.

When Louie Carrillo was fired as an air traffic controller in 1982, he quickly turned his sights to the Amway business he had already halfheartedly begun. "I made a list of 500 people I would try to get into the business," Louie recalls. Most of the 500 were fellow air traffic controllers in the same fix as he. "They all said no. Everybody said no. 'Nobody does Amway,' they told me."

To Louie—who has since built an Executive Diamond–level business with his wife, Kathy—those rejections made him feel all the more responsible for those who said yes. They became part of the Carrillo family. "When a family says yes to you, it's a seed in your hands," he says. "It can grow or it can dry up and blow away. Every seed is a family. Every circle is a family."

Amway provided Chiffi Osbaldi with the love and support of a family when he had no family. That's why he could travel halfway around the world, stand on a stage before people he had never met, look them in the eye, and tell them, "Now I have *you* as my family." Even though he conveyed his feelings through an interpreter, the depth of emotion behind the declaration of the 27-year-old from Indonesia needed no translation. The assembled audience of Amway distributors sat in rapt attention as Chiffi described his escape from the poverty of Jakarta.

"I don't come from a rich family," he told them. "I was good in school, but the friends I chose were a bad influence on me. I got drunk most of the time and liked to smoke. When I first heard about Amway, I didn't sign up because I couldn't afford the kit. So I saved my money until I could afford it."

Chiffi set out to sign up all his friends and discovered that he was good at presenting the Amway Plan. "I was so excited that I went right away to my parents' home to get them involved in the business too. My mother and brother joined immediately."

The young man's father was another matter. He reacted angrily to the business. "Amway over now!" he ordered his family. Chiffi's mother and brother quit. The father and son argued violently, until Chiffi was ordered locked out of the family home forever.

It was a crushing blow. The young man had gone home because the respect of his father was so important to him; instead, he was all but disowned. "I had $10 in my pocket," he said. "I thought, 'That's it for my whole life,' but I knew I had to be responsible for my own dreams." And like everyone who has ever achieved success, he worked hard and refused to give into the demon of self-pity.

Chiffi vowed to show the Plan one hundred times a month for four months: "My dream was very, very strong."

The young man climbed quickly to Silver and then to Emerald. Learning of his success, his family welcomed Chiffi back into his family home and his father's arms.

* * *

Sometimes it's wanting to do right by your adopted Amway family that keeps you going. Not letting down those who have done so much to help you can be a powerful motivating force. For Don and Nancy Wilson of Utah, it made all the difference.

"There are two keys to the success Nancy and I have experienced in this business," Don says. "First, my dad taught me how to work hard. Second, Dexter Yager taught me how to work smart. I don't think a person can be very successful without some of each!"

Working hard was never an issue. Don had played basketball and baseball in college and later became a popular high school teacher and basketball coach. Nancy tried to combine a career in nursing with that of homemaker.

"We realized that we desperately wanted to beat the mental and financial bondage that most people live their lives under," Nancy says. It wasn't easy. When they were introduced to Amway, they knew it represented the path to a better life, but they didn't have the time or the training to get it rolling. However, it is not for nothing that Crown Ambassadors Dexter and Birdie Yager are known as "master dream-builders."

"A three-year-old wants everything," Dexter has said, "but people keep telling him he has to wait. By the time he's in his late teens or early twenties, the world has beat him so bad on what he can't get and can't do that he doesn't dream or set goals anymore. He just lives from week to week. We help people get their dream glands going again. If you dream big, you're going to work hard to get it!"

Don recalls, "The one thing that kept us going was that Dexter and Birdie Yager entered the picture when we started building our business. Once we developed a relationship with them, we knew we could never give up—no matter how difficult it might become. One, we couldn't quit on ourselves. Two, we couldn't quit on Dexter and Birdie. We had too much respect for them to give up."

Today, Don and Nancy Wilson are Executive Diamonds with a worldwide organization. Like Dexter and Birdie Yager, the Wilsons place a great emphasis on teaching and inspiring those who have joined *their* Amway family.

* * *

As you can see, mentors can become like family to provide guidance and support to help their younger or less experienced associates. And Amway is in no short supply of good mentors. Rich DeVos has called Bill Britt "one of the greatest mentors in the history of our company." Bill calls what he does "father power."

It's a gift Bill himself was denied as a boy. His father was an alcoholic. "He was a good man when he was sober," Bill told Rich, "but under the influence everything changed. He kept our family in total chaos."

As a senior in high school, Bill worked nights at a gas station in Daytona Beach, Florida. There were times when he actually had to guard the cash register from his own father, who, when drunk, would sometimes come in search of money.

"I had no time for sports or for all-school events like concerts or dances. I had no time for friends and, worse, I never learned to study. I never took a book home; I did just enough to pass and somehow escaped high school with a diploma."

Following high school, though, Bill was accepted into the U.S. Army's Officer Candidate School. He achieved the rank of lieutenant and served in the Korean War. Returning to his native North Carolina, he put himself through college with the help of the GI Bill and earned a degree in engineering. Later, with the help of his father-in-law, he began a career in city government.

Bill Britt was denied the mentoring of his father, but he found it in many other sources as he and his wife, Peggy, built their Amway business: his grandmother, his comrades in arms, his father-in-law, and in Jesus Christ.

Father power. "In this business, we could call it father and mother power," Bill explains. "We upline 'dads' and 'moms' must learn to parent our downline 'sons' and 'daughters.' Like good parents, we rejoice when our children grow up, when they become our peers, and when they go on to do even better than we have done."

By that score, Crown Bernice Hansen-Gilbert has done a great deal of rejoicing through her nearly half-century association with Jay Van Andel and Rich DeVos. She and her late husband, Fred, sold Nutrilite products in the 1950s and joined Amway literally at the basement level. Since then, Bernice has provided thousands of Amway distributors with motherly guidance and counsel as they have climbed through the ranks.

PASSING DOWN A LEGACY

Having been in operation now for 37 years, Amway is at the stage where many successful distributors and the company itself are placing their legacies in the hands of a new generation. "There's a lot of second-generation people now getting involved in the business," Brian Hays told me. "Our kids were raised in it."

Brian adds, "Most of us parents sponsor our children at zero. Let them slug it out for themselves. Sure, one day they'll inherit the businesses, but right now the best course is to throw them into the living rooms to show the Plan. That's what most of us do." And it's a wise course, one that the kids will undoubtedly thank their parents for—later!

Triple Diamonds Jerry and Cherry Meadows are proud that their son and daughter have joined them in the business. It's the ultimate payoff for an odyssey that began in 1970. "At age 26, Jerry had ulcers and was working 80 hours a week," Cherry recalls. "I didn't want our little boy to grow up not knowing his dad. I saw a business we could do together."

Jerry kept thinking about his father. "My dad always wanted his own business, so it became a goal of mine. And I saw people with better educations—master's and doctorate degrees—lose their jobs because of industry changes."

The Meadows' successful business freed them from that corporate trap and pulled their family together. Today, Jerry and Cherry and their son and daughter are all involved in their business. "When kids work together with their parents," Jerry says, "it builds understanding and values more than just playing together does."

Amway Corporation itself is enjoying new strength in the next generation, as the founders and their children work together for future success. The DeVos and Van Andel children will tell you that they've been much luckier than other children of successful businesspeople. The history of family-owned business empires is replete with stories of second-generation playboys and playgirls indulging themselves in the fast lane of life, squandering money and engaging in self-destructive behavior. Some "sow the wild oats" for a time and then expect to come sailing right into the CEO's chair as soon as Daddy retires.

But the DeVos and Van Andel children have had a very different experience. They have all had to work hard in the business. Daughter Nan Van Andel has said, "We all remember the reason that we're all here today is because of the hard work those guys [Rich and Jay] put in at the beginning. This isn't something that just gets handed to you. Us kids remember that."

Nan remembers something else too: "I'll never forget it. I sold a hundred dollars' worth of products and I got a believer's pin, and I'll tell you, that was exciting to me. Recognition is something that so many people don't have. We have it here in the Amway business."

That sums up the spirit and the ethic instilled in the DeVos and Van Andel children. Since the 1970s, all eight children have helped build distributorships and have performed a variety of tasks in Amway Corporation. No job has been considered too small or beneath them.

In 1992, Rich and Jay took the next step. They created the Amway Policy Board, which is the leadership team that now guides the company. It's a family affair: the board consists of the dads and their children. While the Amway Policy Board will chart the company's strategic course, the day-to-day management and leadership are now in the hands of the two eldest sons, Dick DeVos and

Steve Van Andel. Dick became president of Amway in January 1993, following his father's retirement at age 66.

Jay Van Andel's retirement from his day-to-day role in the company in September 1995 at the age of 71 completed Amway's transition to a second generation of leadership. Steve Van Andel assumed the post of chairman and, together with Dick DeVos, resides in the office of chief executive.

One question the founders and their sons are frequently asked is this: Will the Dick/Steve team function as famously as the Rich/Jay team has for over half a century? "Jay and I have been friends and business partners for more than 50 years," Rich DeVos told a newspaper last year. "That's a rare achievement in business, but we're confident that Dick and Steve will work together in the same spirit of this partnership. I've watched Steve grow up in the Amway business. I'm confident he has the experience and the ability to capably succeed Jay."

Says Steve of his partner: "Dick and I have known each other our entire lives. We've learned business together as well as lived business together. Over the last couple of years, both of us spent a lot of time in Asia." Dick DeVos echoes this sentiment, noting that "we've had a personal relationship that goes back to the fact that we grew up next door to each other."

Barely 40 years old, these young men face a unique challenge. After all, how would *you* like to try to fill the shoes of Rich DeVos and Jay Van Andel? In July 1995, the new team sat down with the *Detroit News*, and Dick described the challenge this way: "What you see is a company on a great course. It's hard to argue with the success that my father and Jay had. We want to continue to be the industry leader. We would like to see a company that brings into acceptance the direct-selling concept to the marketplace."

For his part, Steve Van Andel describes a deliberate approach to leading Amway: "What we have done is look over the past years at how my dad and Rich had their partnership over 50 years. They established some of the foundations for the business with their values. Although we're different people, we expect to continue with a similar partnership."

The words of the new partners may sound humble, but Amway's future will surely be bold. A recent *Amagram* message to Amway distributors, issued by cofounders Rich DeVos and Jay Van Andel, discussed the future and set forth four goals in particular:

- The Amway of the future must maintain a viable and attractive business opportunity.
- The Amway of the future must increase its bias toward action.
- The Amway of the future will require more creativity than ever.
- The Amway of the future will measure success in more than economic terms.

"We believe Amway has the potential to double in size in the next five years," Rich and Jay continue, "but that will not happen automatically. It will require a dedicated effort on the part of distributors and employees worldwide to continue our tradition of growth, innovation, and success. Steve and Dick, the Amway Policy

Board, and the Amway management team have an unswerving commitment to continue these traditions."

Amway sons and daughters throughout the business have tremendous tools and resources at hand to lead both the corporation and thousands of solid family businesses capably into the next century. But this is also a business that respects the wisdom of age. Of all the assets at their disposal, there is little question that Dick and Steve would tell you that the most precious of them all is . . . Rich and Jay. The strong, reassuring hands of the fathers on the shoulders of the sons will continue as long as God is willing.

5

Against All Odds

There are three kinds of handicaps in life: the ones we're born with, the ones imposed on us by others, and the ones we impose on ourselves.

You'd think that the handicaps we're born with would be the hardest to overcome. But then you read about people like Amy Van Dyken, an asthmatic, winning *four* Olympic gold medals in swimming at the 1996 games. You'd also think that belonging to the "wrong" ethnic group would deny you the fruits of success. But then you watch Colin Powell address in prime time the convention of a major political party that had tried to make him its presidential candidate.

Although it would seem that external forces determine our destiny, in reality, it is most often the limitations we impose on ourselves that are the biggest obstacles to overcome. Amy Van Dyken, Colin Powell, and millions of others have succeeded despite real and perceived handicaps because they have refused to limit their will to achieve their dreams.

The essence of the Amway business is to insist that no matter how long the odds, people can find the inner power to do great things. As Crown Ambassador Dexter

Yager once said, "An excuse is the skin of a lie, stuffed with a reason."

Unlike any other business opportunity I have ever seen, Amway gives people the strength to succeed in the face of incredible odds. Some people even credit the business with saving their lives.

HIGHS AND LOWS

Among those who consider their Amway success as a lifesaver is a 34-year-old Diamond from Southern California. His story is so personal that he and his wife prefer that I not use their real names. I'm going to call them Bill and Mary.

Bill was popular in school and seemed headed for success. "I was preparing to be a champion," he told me. "But I also lived the party life and I crossed the line. I became obsessed with drugs and alcohol and became totally addicted. Before I knew it, I was broken as a man. Mary and I led separate lives. We almost got divorced, and thoughts of suicide crossed my mind."

Amway was virtually the only positive force in a life of despair. "I grew up in the Amway business, starting at age 24," Bill says. "I was living two lives, and building the Amway business was my positive life; at the same time, I was leading a negative life of alcohol and drugs, undergoing a terrible internal struggle that few people knew about."

Eventually, people found out. "The people in the business didn't condone what I was doing, but they wanted to help me get through it. They offered their love and their care. You can see why Amway is more than a business to us—it's an extended family."

"This is a business that tolerates mistakes," Bill told me. "If I were in the corporate world, I would have been fired and cut off from my source of income, and the blemishes would be there on my resume forever."

Bill hastens to note that Amway offered no miracle cure. After all, his addictions continued and grew worse even as he and Mary began building their business. The business, however, gave them the tools to turn their lives around and a support system to stay afloat in a sea of turmoil. "This business continued to provide me with income even when I couldn't be there. It's a business that really cares about people."

Today, a clean and sober Bill and his wife are new Diamonds, building a business that has spawned more than 20 Direct Distributors in Southern California, over 1,000 distributors in China, and a strong presence in the Midwest and in Eastern Europe. "I never even considered a global dimension to my business or my life when I first started in Amway," Bill says. "Those are the kinds of doors Amway opens for you."

APOCALYPSE THEN, AMWAY NOW

John and Maria Herren began their lives on opposite ends of a world just recovering from the devastation of World War II. Maria was born in Tokyo to a Japanese mother and an American father. John was born in Italy to an Italian mother and an American father. Both emigrated to the United States as children.

Maria in particular recalls the sting of ridicule and discrimination. In Japan, they said she wasn't really Japanese; in America, she was told she was not a real American. That, coupled with the reserved nature of her Japanese upbringing, made Maria very shy. "I used to call it shyness," Maria says, "but shyness is really fear, and fear is false evidence appearing real."

On the other side of the world, John Herren's father had disappeared, but the young boy nonetheless benefited from the love and support of a big Italian family. They dreamed of going to America; to pay for the journey, John's grandfather put a big black kettle in the corner of the house. Every time they could, they threw a few coins in the pot. "When the pot is filled," John's grandfather told him, "we're going to America."

And they did. John says he will never forget his first glimpse of the Statue of Liberty through the porthole of the ship that carried him to America.

Given his background, John felt he had a lot to prove in America. He was driven by a fierce competitiveness—and more than a little anger and aggressiveness. "I was always ready to fight," John remembers. "I just knew I had to be the best and never quit. Why? Because I had to look my grandfather in the face."

After high school, John "won the only lottery I ever won—the draft lottery." Faced with the inevitable, he enlisted in the paratroopers and later found himself on Hamburger Hill in Vietnam, the scene of one of the bloodiest battles of that terrible war.

It was a turning point. John came back from the war gripped by fears and anxieties. He took medication to calm himself down and then amphetamines to lift himself up.

One day, he was hanging out on the beach in Monterey, California, drinking wine and staring out at the ocean. He fell sound asleep until he was awakened by a young woman poking him in the back. The woman was Maria.

With Maria by his side, John pulled himself out of self-pity. He made it through college and got an MBA. "There was only one problem," he reports. "I had no business to be a master in!"

Then John and Maria were shown the Amway Plan. They were skeptical at first. "I didn't understand it. I didn't believe it," John says. "But I thought I'd buy a few products because I felt obligated, and that would be the end of it."

Maria was just plain scared. "It was very difficult for me," she remembers. "I didn't think I could do it. I used every excuse possible not to do this business."

Nonetheless, they tried. They poured themselves into it, becoming Silver Producers four months into the business. They reached Pearl in thirteen months and Emerald six months after that. Today, Maria proudly sums up the couple's remarkable achievement: "We were two people from different ends of the world and from totally different backgrounds who made it to Diamond. I gained self-confidence from the business. I have friends all over the world. I wouldn't trade my life for anything!"

For John, there's no question that Amway has helped him overcome the handicaps within. Recalling the scars of his Vietnam experience, he says, "I had to think of something to keep me sane in the midst of all that insanity." He is convinced that the business is an ideal home for other veterans who have been through similar searing experiences. "It's a wonderful way for veterans to come back into society in a positive way instead of wallowing in self-pity."

Given John's wartime torment, I was somewhat reluctant to mention to him that I had recently spent a lot of time in Vietnam, even producing an encouraging book about the country's business opportunities. While acknowledging that a visit to postwar Vietnam would be an emotional experience, he enthusiastically focused on the potential I described for an Amway bonanza in the country. I told him I would be honored to travel there with him.

For all that their business has done for the Herrens, perhaps the richest reward came when John was reunited with the father he never knew. "I was scheduled to make a speech to a large rally," he told me. "My father heard about it and showed up. He left when I was one-and-a-half years old. I hadn't seen him in 48 years. Now we have begun a new relationship. And it's all because of this business."

DROPOUT DREAMS

André Blanchard of Montreal will not have *that* chance. "As a result of illness, my father became an invalid at the age of 35," he explains. "He died 10 years later, leaving my mother penniless with five children, no insurance whatsoever, and many debts.

"I was 12 at the time and I was forced to quit school and go to work. I promised myself then that when I had a family of my own, I would never make them go through what my family had experienced."

Easier said than done! In 1967, André was making $70 a week as a supervisor for a wholesale grocery chain. "As for my skills, all I could offer on my résumé was a seventh-grade education, and French was the only language I could speak, read, or write." When André and his wife, Françoise, heard about the Amway Plan, André was eager to learn more.

Françoise was another matter. Somehow, André convinced Françoise to accompany him to a meeting. "The long drive was done in silence," he recalls. "The only reason she came was to protect me. Her reaction was even stronger when she reached the meeting place and she saw a black Cadillac with New York license plates parked in front of the house where we were going." Françoise's deep mistrust transferred to André. As they entered the house, "we both had the feeling we had been taken in and were going to be the victim of con artists," André remembers.

Yet, to his surprise, the meeting, which featured an enthusiastic French-American from Syracuse, completely turned him around: "I was so wound up, I could hardly contain myself."

It was slow going at first. Françoise was still not on board, and prospects kept quitting on André. He recalls an early meeting with 40 candidates—they all left without joining. The last one to leave said, "André, you'll be good at this."

He kept at it, and within months he was earning more from Amway than he was from his job. That helped turn Françoise around. The turning point came when André asked his boss for unpaid vacation in order to attend a Direct Distributor's seminar in Michigan. The

boss refused, and André quit. Within 16 months, André—
with Françoise now by his side in the Amway business—
became Diamonds.

Today, the man with the seventh-grade education
and the woman who struggled so fiercely with her fears
and suspicions, pioneering a business many said would
never work in Quebec, rank among the most successful
Amway distributors anywhere and among the most successful businesspeople in Canada. The couple's four
children are all following in their parents' footsteps. The
Blanchards' business operates in more than 15 countries, with an organization estimated at more than
100,000 distributors.

Only in this business could a man who never graduated from high school today be looked up to as a *teacher*
equipping others with the skills and tools they need to
succeed and stand on their own. Through his publishing
company and other activities, André Blanchard fervently
spreads the gospel of the business approach that has
enabled him to overcome such long odds.

About network marketing, he has written:

You are in business for yourself.

You are the boss.

You make up your own schedule.

Your territory has no boundaries.

You sponsor where you want and live where you want.

You do not need employees.

You choose the people with whom you want to build
your business.

You do not need any money for luxurious office space.

You have tax benefits.

There are no accounts receivable.

You develop your own leadership and personal skills.

You build your own business, one that you can pass on to your legal heirs.

You distribute quality products and services.

André and Françoise Blanchard prove that in the Amway business where you came from won't keep you from where you want to go.

PRIDE AND PREJUDICE

For a long time, Ruth Halsey measured her success by the number of rooms in her house. She and her husband, George, started married life in a mobile home. They worked their way to a five-room house, then a seven-room house, then a dream house with fourteen rooms. But as the number of rooms grew, so did the Halseys' debts. "I acted like I actually had money," Ruth has said.

She also had a tremendous drive to succeed. The third of seven children growing up in an African-American family in Greensboro, North Carolina, Ruth had "always wanted to be great in everything I did. We had nothing but each other, but we had big dreams."

George grew up in Wilmington, North Carolina, "in an area they called 'the ghetto.'" From the beginning, he was determined to free himself from that existence. He made it to North Carolina State University but still found opportunities limited. He worked in a mattress factory, then in a textile plant making pajamas. He swept floors in an insurance company and did a stint walking a beat as a cop.

Settling into married life, George found a job as a claims adjuster for an insurance company and stuck with it for more than six years. Ruth taught school. The houses kept getting bigger—so did the bills.

One day, one of George's coworkers told him about Amway. Everyone else in the office warned him against it. Ruth was decidedly negative as well, but she could offer no other avenue to follow to achieve their dreams, except the thin hope of "winning the *Reader's Digest* contest."

When they went to Amway functions, Ruth recalls "seeing no blacks crossing that stage." To George, the fact that friends both black and white were telling him that "blacks can't make it in Amway" made him all the more determined to prove them wrong.

"We had to do it. There was no choice. There was nothing out there," George recalls. "I had to do it for my people. I had to let them know it was for real. They laughed at me. They don't laugh anymore."

No, they don't. From 1975 to today, the Halseys have built their business to the Triple Diamond level. Ruth has even added more rooms to the house! "Now I've got a distributor room, a product room, and an office," she says. "And I've got a full-time husband. Things just keep on happening. This business has done so much for us. We've come a long way, baby!"

ESCAPE FROM THE BARRIOS . . .
AND THE BOARDROOMS

The son of Mexican immigrants, Frank Morales was born in the sugar beet fields of Nebraska. His older brother and sister were felled by disease and never made it past infancy. Growing up in a three-room house without running water in a poor Mexican neighborhood of Kansas City, Kansas, Frank's early life was defined by poverty, prejudice, and segregation.

Frank attended a high school that was predominantly white. He immediately faced prejudice there—starting with his teacher! "On the first day, she told me, 'You Mexicans belong with the blacks across town.' She didn't say 'black,' though."

School at first was marked by numerous fistfights and controversies. He even wound up in jail at age 14. Tagged as a troublemaker, Frank realized he had to straighten himself out. He performed well in his studies and in athletics. He began developing his persuasive skills to overcome the roadblocks thrown in his path. On numerous occasions, he talked himself into restaurants and nightclubs that excluded Mexicans by befriending the managers. He refused to let poverty and prejudice beat him down.

"My mother asked me whether I would ever be satisfied with what I had. I said no. I started seeing the difference between the haves and the have-nots."

Then, suddenly, Frank's family had nothing. A flood washed away their small house. They moved to Kansas City, Missouri, where Frank and friends plunged themselves into entrepreneurship. They started a band that played at weddings and parties. Frank started booking other bands. At one function, he met his high school sweetheart and future wife, Barbara.

When an opportunity presented itself to begin a career in the relatively new field of data processing, Frank jumped at it. Barbara worked in a bank. The young married couple began climbing the corporate ladder, enjoying success that eventually took them to California.

Frank Morales freed himself from the traps that had been set for him. He climbed out of childhood poverty and rose above prejudice, all the way to a senior position for a Fortune 500 company. Barbara Morales found similar success and status in her banking career. The American Dream had triumphed once again.

But it wasn't enough. Something was missing. Frank told me of being astonished by the fact that after 27 years in the corporate world, he barely had $2,000 in the bank. Barbara worried about the future of her marriage. "I feared that we might end up getting divorced once our four children were grown," she said.

Then they heard about Amway. Cocky and confident, they decided to give it a try, figuring that as experienced corporate executives, "we'll tear this thing up. We'll be Diamonds in three days."

It didn't happen in three days, but it happened. Successful and happy, Frank and Barbara take particular pleasure in the success and happiness they bring to others through Amway. "You may think this is a product business, but it is really a people business," Frank told me. "It's all about helping individuals realize their dreams."

A BUSINESS FOR EVERYONE

- Leslie and Myra Lambeth of Michigan are hearing-impaired. They're making it in Amway by having their families and uplines help them present the Plan.
- Dick Ossinger of Washington is blind. With his wife, Dee, by his side, he is making it in Amway.
- P. J. Carey of Oklahoma is 76 years old. She's making it in Amway, having started her business at the ripe young age of 74. "I'll sleep at the cemetery," she says.
- And from the chatter on the Web comes this message: "I'm a distributor from Florida. I'm having a ball building this business. I am also a paraplegic—for 25 years. I had a motorcycle wreck at 18 and severed my spine. If I can build this business, anyone can build it."

With the sound of doors slamming shut all around us in today's economy, Amway opens its doors to all. Here is a business that asks "What can you contribute?" not "What is your résumé?" It seeks the best of us, and it asks us to leave behind our excuses for not breaking out of our own self-imposed limitations.

This self-driving spirit is the lifeblood of Roger Crawford, author of *Playing from the Heart* (Prima). Born with severe and very visible birth defects that affected his upper and lower limbs, Roger overcame the tremendous odds and became a professional tennis player. "The only difference between you and me," he is fond of saying, "is that you can see my handicap but I cannot see yours."

People who live with disabilities, prejudice, poverty, limited education, and other roadblocks to fulfillment are finding a home in Amway. So can "ordinary" people like you and me, who live with self-imposed limitations but are aching to break out of them. The Amway opportunity shines its light of hope even in the darkest of places. That speaks volumes about the character of this business and the people in it.

6

The Measure of Success

Success is the progressive realization of a worthwhile dream.

—Dexter Yager

Bruce Kanegai has been successful at almost everything he has ever done—and he has done almost everything!

This Amway Direct Distributor has taught art in a Southern California high school for 25 years. An expert in karate, he teaches classes at night and has instructed the Beverly Hills Police Department and other law enforcement officers on survival techniques. He's an expert skier and has set records in hiking and backpacking, which he also teaches. It's been a full, busy, and confident life for Bruce and his wife, Nancy, who has also had a career in teaching.

So why have they carved out the necessary time to build a successful Amway business? "We both wanted to take our teaching to a more positive level," Bruce says. "Teaching is where my calling is, and that's what I'm doing in this business."

And doing it well! Bruce reports that he already brings in more income from Amway than he does from 25 years of high school teaching. That has enabled

Nancy to leave her full-time job and focus on their Amway business and their children.

He has great respect for the tough challenges facing law enforcement, "but it's kind of nice to get out of the environment of all the four-letter words and into a more positive, uplifting environment."

Bruce has little patience for those who say they have no time for Amway. "I teach school all day, pick up the kids, go teach a karate class at night, and still make it to the kitchens and living rooms to show the Amway Plan," he says.

The Kanegais also take pride in living up to the legacies of their ancestors. Bruce is a Japanese-American whose grandparents arrived in San Francisco in 1904 and later established a successful family business in the section of Los Angeles known as Little Tokyo. Nancy is a descendant of the captain of the Mayflower. "Both our families came to America for the same reason—freedom and free enterprise," Bruce says. "They just came here at different times and from different parts of the world."

The Kanegais' story both raises and helps answer one of the most frequently asked questions about Amway: What does success really mean in the Amway business?

Some critics of this business like to define the terms of success narrowly and superficially by asking these questions: How many people really make it? Is it realistic to think that the average person will be able to achieve their financial goals? In this way, they can attack the credibility of the business. Their line of attack goes something like this:

1. Amway distributors are enticed to sign on by the promise of a life of great wealth and leisure.
2. Few people actually achieve that kind of success.
3. Therefore, most people fail, and the business is a fraud.

Harsh words? Yes. It's suspicion born of ignorance and narrow-minded thinking. But there isn't a successful Amway distributor out there who has not heard all this and worse.

Do Bruce and Nancy Kanegai dream of the day they make it to the Crown level of distributorship with all the accompanying incentives that achievement brings? Of course they do. But that is not the only way they measure success. Even if they never made one additional dollar from their Amway business, Bruce and Nancy will tell you that they have found success in important ways:

- Bruce finds that their Amway business provides an environment that is more positive than the rough world of law enforcement.
- The couple has a new outlet to pursue the true calling of their lives—that of helping others through teaching.
- The family has freed itself from the morass of credit card debt that has consumed so many families.
- Nancy has more time to spend with the children.
- Bruce has been able to be true to the legacy of his immigrant grandparents, who left everything behind in Japan to pursue their dream of free enterprise.

The Kanegais have yet to become rich in the Amway business. But in so many ways they have become *enriched*. Isn't that a better standard of achievement?

* * *

As a Crown Ambassador, Dan Williams would certainly fit most definitions of having achieved financial independence. He was successful in Amway right off the bat, and, at age 70, he hasn't stopped or slowed down. But when you talk to Dan Williams about his success in the business, his thoughts invariably turn not to money but to the stutter that has marked his speech since he was five years old.

Despite the humiliation he suffered, Dan plunged on ahead with life, serving admirably as a Navy lieutenant and successfully as an executive with Dow Chemical. The worst thing was the lengths to which he felt tempted to go to avoid introducing himself and his wife, Bunny, to other people. "The D's and the B's were the hardest. It was really humiliating."

Today, there's but a faint echo of the stutter that was such a struggle for Dan Williams. Dan credits Amway. His speech improved markedly as he poured his energies into the business. "It improved when I got my mind off myself and onto other people."

* * *

The measure of success. It's as unique as your dreams or mine. For Dan Williams, success was being able to introduce Bunny without fear or embarrassment. Diamond Direct Distributor Henry Zampa of Michigan simply wanted to buy a 30-foot sailboat!

"When Carol and I started out in Amway, my only goal was to get that boat," Henry said. "Well, about three months later, I went sailing!" Mission accomplished. On that level, the business delivered precisely what the Zampas asked it to.

"I have no boat now," Henry continues. "My values have changed. My goal now is to help people. I get more satisfaction from that than I do from sailing.

"You have to grow personally to grow in the business," he says. "There are many ways of making money, but there's no other way to develop a lifestyle and make friends the world over, like you can here."

* * *

Diamond Direct Distributor Carla Wilson of California says she used to be a small thinker: "I didn't want a career. My dream was to get married, raise a family, and stay home."

That dream remains at the center of Carla's life, but she thinks small no more. "You can achieve anything you want in life through this business," she says, "but maybe it's not the money that's important."

Carla's husband, Mike, had enjoyed plenty of success and popularity in his life; what he lacked was meaning and direction. Growing up was pretty easy for Mike: "I was your basic all-American kid." But when Mike hit college, the sense of drifting and aimlessness set in. "I obviously had a goal of being a flake," he says. "I felt like my life was in a tailspin. I was trying to find something I wanted to do with my life.

"I knew this much: Life had to be more than working five days a week to enjoy two days a week."

Mike thought he found his calling when he became a successful world class tennis pro, competing on the international circuit and later teaching at several posh country clubs in Southern California. But the grind of teaching from 7 A.M. to 10 P.M. pulled him and Carla apart. A goal had been reached and a measure of success had been achieved, but Mike was fundamentally unhappy—even "borderline suicidal." He felt that he had lost control of his life, and he needed to find a change.

When he saw the Amway Plan, he didn't like it at first, but he resolved to be "the guy that's gonna do this." And he did.

The financial rewards, welcome as they are, fade into the background as Mike and Carla evaluate what Amway has done for their lives. "We have received many of the finest material blessings," Mike says, "but the freedom to have complete control over our lives is very special and priceless."

*   *   *

How does one measure success when you've been a star athlete enjoying the adulation of the crowd? Former NFL player and now Triple Diamond Tim Foley played for the Miami Dolphins for 11 seasons under coach Don Shula. He was part of the team that won the 1973 Super Bowl after the Dolphins' historic undefeated season.

Tim knew it would not last forever: "It doesn't take a rocket scientist to realize that fame is temporary," he has said. "I knew I wasn't going to play for the Dolphins until I was 65." He and his wife, Connie, considered and tried a series of ventures that they believed could provide both an interesting challenge and financial security once the roar of the crowds stopped ringing in their ears. None of them worked.

Tim's thoughts turned back to his boyhood and the small amusement park his father managed during the summers and on weekends in Skokie, Illinois. "My father was a staunchly independent human being," he remembers. "Like his father and his grandfather before him, my father had the entrepreneurial spirit. He had to work for himself. It was the tradition in which he had been raised."

As a boy at the amusement park, Tim kept that tradition alive, selling refreshments, toys, and trinkets to other children. He vividly recalls that even though his father owned the park, no task around the grounds was beneath him: "He wanted to be sure that his customers were never disappointed."

So after a most spectacular interlude of fame on the football field, Tim Foley, with Connie by his side, set out to redefine the meaning of success in their lives. Today, they own a very successful Amway business.

* * *

Back in the late 1960s, Hal and Susan Gooch of Thomasville, North Carolina, weren't thinking about life after fame. They were thinking about how to pay off their bills and move out of their $55-a-month rental.

Hal worked for his father's small furniture company. Susan worked as a computer operator. Most of the families in this small town derived their livelihoods from the Thomasville Furniture Company, which was owned by the Finch family.

The Finches lived in a huge mansion, and the Gooches used to drive out to it and stand under a big oak tree and dream of the day when they could live in a house like that. Throughout the ensuing years of backbreaking work and perseverance, the image of that house—not for what it was but what it represented—came to define their dreams.

Today, Hal and Susan Gooch have paid their bills. They did it by building a successful Amway business to the Double Diamond level, a business that operates in all 50 states and in over 50 countries. And, yes, they live in a beautiful home.

* * *

When they began building their Amway business, Billy and Peggy Florence of Georgia measured success very simply. They wanted to replace Peggy's teaching salary so that they could begin a family. Billy's salary as an Air Force pilot just wasn't enough.

Today, as Executive Diamonds, the Florences have achieved financial rewards and material comforts far beyond their original goals. But that's not how they measure success today.

"Sure, the travel is nice, as is owning my own airplane," Billy says. "But the greatest parts of this business are *unseen* things—being around Dexter Yager and the other Diamonds. No amount of money could buy the wisdom you get from those times. And of course, there is no dollar value for the freedom we have or for the opportunity to be full-time parents for our children."

Peggy Florence echoes this vision of success: "We are excited to be a part of a growing number of the most innovative, creative, and freedom-loving people in the world."

* * *

Executive Diamond Bill Childers has thought a lot about how you define success in the Amway business. After all, he was already a professional success when he worked his way up in a variety of jobs to a solid position in the steel industry. But it wasn't enough, and so in

1973 he began to build a business. "I realized that I was going to have to get into personal business ownership if I was ever going to achieve financial independence," Bill recalls. Today, Bill's Childers Enterprises group operates all over the world. Yet he hasn't forgotten what it's like just starting out—all those questions, all those doubts, all those dreams.

"Not long after getting into the business," Bill remembers, "I went to my first major function. There was so much that happened that weekend to inspire and motivate me, to literally change my life. I'll never forget that during a break, I sat beside the motel pool dreaming about the future, and I began wondering what it would feel like to have a hundred people in my group attend a function together.

"It's so incredible now to look around and see the measures of success those within our organization have attained."

For those who think all the opportunities in network marketing have already been spoken for, Bill Childers offers some wise advice: "There's more opportunity now than when I got involved in 1973. There are numerous new products, more great tools, more credibility, and certainly more technology at our fingertips. Still, it all comes down to what's in your heart."

* * *

The measure of success. For some, it's becoming a millionaire. For others, it's being able to earn enough extra income to pay off bills or make that special purchase of a car, boat, or home.

For yet others, the goal is to bring families drifting apart back together. Or, the dream is about enabling a spouse to be at home with the children in an era when too many of our children are alone and at risk.

Some join the business to make new friends, to help others succeed, or to teach and mentor young people.

Some join so they can stand on their own. Others join because they want to be part of a team.

Some join so they can improve their quality of life. Others do it in the hopes of building a secure retirement.

Some join with nothing to prove, having already achieved great success in other occupations. Some join with everything to prove: "I'm the one who can make this work!"

When Diamond Direct Distributor Jay Cuccia of California speaks of Amway as "a melting pot just like America, a business of tremendous diversity," he's not talking simply about race, religion, or ethnic background. He's talking about dreams, about the way we each measure success in our own lives. That's why the critics who seek to evaluate Amway simply in terms of how many people strike it rich are missing the entire point of the business.

Amway has and never will hold out the false promise of instant wealth. Rather, it offers something far more valuable: a lifetime of choices and possibilities.

* * *

Let's talk very plainly and practically about money.

It's worth remembering that even modest sums of additional income—if handled responsibly—can, with patience and perseverance, lead to a more secure and bountiful life. Let's assume, very conservatively, that you earn 6 percent interest on annual deposits of the entire year's proceeds from your Amway business. (The following exercise would apply regardless of the source of income.)

If you save $300 yearly ($25 average monthly savings), you'd have:

- $1,691 after 5 years
- $3,954 after 10 years
- $6,983 after 15 years
- $11,036 after 20 years

If you save $900 yearly ($75 average monthly savings), you'd have:

- $5,073 after 5 years
- $15,109 after 10 years
- $20,948 after 15 years
- $33,107 after 20 years

If you save $1,800 yearly ($150 average monthly savings), you'd have:

- $10,147 after 5 years
- $30,218 after 10 years
- $41,897 after 15 years
- $66,214 after 20 years

If you save $6,000 yearly ($500 average monthly savings), you'd have:

- $33,823 after 5 years
- $100,726 after 10 years
- $139,656 after 15 years
- $220,714 after 20 years

If you save $12,000 yearly ($1,000 average monthly savings), you'd have:

- $67,645 after 5 years
- $201,452 after 10 years
- $279,312 after 15 years
- $441,427 after 20 years

Of course, should you save or invest your extra income at a higher rate of return, your "paltry" monthly sums would grow that much more. For example, at 8 percent interest, your $6,000 in yearly savings would provide you with a nest egg of:

- $35,200 after 5 years
- $107,074 after 10 years
- $162,913 after 15 years
- $274,572 after 20 years

And if you are able to sock away $12,000 a year at 8 percent, you'd have:

- $70,399 after 5 years
- $214,147 after 10 years
- $325,825 after 15 years
- $549,144 after 20 years

So here is how you *can* become a millionaire. Save $1,200 a month at 12 percent interest, and you'll be one in 20 years, accumulating a nest egg of $1,037,555.

You say you *shouldn't* have to wait that long? You were willing to go deep into debt to go to college for four or six or eight years—so that you could work for somebody else for 30, 40, or 50 years! Why do you so readily accept *that* formula for living but not the one of prudent saving and investment?

You say you want it all right here, right now? Play the lottery. Good luck!

Maybe Amway won't allow you to quit your job and get out of the rut *today*, but there's always tomorrow. The sums of money listed above could determine whether:

- You and your spouse can take that cruise you've always dreamed of to celebrate your twenty-fifth anniversary
- You can retire at 60 instead of 65, or not at all
- You can send your children to the college of their choice
- You can maintain an adequate lifestyle if you get laid off, with a ready-made business there to take its place
- You can qualify for the mortgage to buy the new home you've been dreaming about
- You can live out your years in the homey atmosphere of a Leisure World or assisted living community instead of in a Medicare-supported nursing home
- You bequeath a legacy to your children and your grandchildren

* * *

Amway Executive Diamonds Glen and Joya Baker of California used to believe they could simply spend their way to their dreams. They lived way beyond their means; both worked full time just to pay the mounting bills. Savings? Not a chance.

"I thought I was doing great in the rut system," Glen said of his career in insurance. "My dream was reduced to trying to bring in enough money to pay the $8,000 a month in bills we had piled up.

"Then, in 1989, I got a call from an old high school friend who wanted to show me something he said would 'raise my eyebrows.' It was Amway."

Glen and Joya remember being "completely uninterested" in the Plan. "We blew him off four separate times," Glen told me, "because we thought we knew it all, thought we found it all."

Today the Bakers are thankful that their sponsor kept coming back to them. Once they finally made a commitment to build a business, they immediately set their sights on the Diamond level. "We followed the steps of the World Wide Dreambuilders' system and we did it," Glen said. Today, as Executive Diamonds, Glen and Joya work on their business full time. They successfully freed themselves from the debt trap and rut of nine-to-five careers.

"We had a dream," Glen said, "a tremendous burn to do it. When people put us down, we just got stronger. We knew exactly, on faith, that if we did the work, the results would follow."

* * *

In a reflective conversation several years ago with David John Harris, a graduate student preparing his doctoral dissertation, Rich DeVos and Jay Van Andel talked about the people of Amway and the dreams they have all shared and achieved. Although each person's individual goal may be different, there are common goals that everyone can understand and strive for. Rich observed that regardless of nationality, people "like to eat, they want to live better, they want to be free, they want to travel, they want to take care of their children."

Jay expanded on the theme: "There is a common thread. Rich pointed out some of it. Being able to use the phrase, 'live a better life'—whatever that means to the individual. To most individuals, that means doing just a little better than what they've got now. To one who has nothing, it may mean very little more, but it's more.

"That's the material thing. But it evolves into a great deal more than just material things. There's the desire a great many people have to be able to do things on their own. That's probably fundamental to the entrepreneurial drive. It's one of those things that create an entrepreneur."

People in the Amway business have told me stories that have struck chords in my own life. For example, Crown Ambassadors Jerry and Sharyn Webb of Texas really struggled when Jerry was working on his Ph.D. at the University of Texas. They lived in an Army barrack that had been converted into married students' housing. Roaches were crawling all over the place.

When their daughter was hospitalized due to an illness, they had to borrow $50 to pay the bill before they could take her home. And they recalled that the staple of their diet was boxed macaroni and cheese at 18¢ a box, seven boxes a week.

I remember those boxes well! Just as I was heading off to college, my family back home had undergone some severe crises that destroyed us financially. One semester, I had $7 a week for food. Like the Webbs, I bought those boxes of instant macaroni and cheese, except by then, they were 25¢ a box. I made the sauce with water instead of milk.

"You can appreciate more where you are when you remember where you came from," Jerry says. After he became successful in Amway, he recalls that "for years I couldn't eat macaroni and cheese."

I still can't. And I don't have to. For me, that's a measure of success.

7

Going Global

Most of us fortunate enough to visit the beautiful Hawaiian islands have little but fun, sun, sand, and surf on our minds. When Diamond Direct Distributor Linda Agus was there, she worried about postage stamps.

She and her husband, Paul, were visiting the islands recently, along with thousands of Amway distributors, including a large group from Indonesia. For many in this group, it was the first time they had left their homeland and the first time they had visited the United States.

Linda was concerned, because this group had already scrimped and saved to make the trip. Some carried packages of instant noodles in their luggage so they could save on meals. Knowing how much they would want to relate their experiences to relatives back home in Indonesia, she decided to help them out by buying 600 postage stamps, at 50¢ each, for postcards. It was a wonderful gesture on her part, but when she canvassed the group to find out how many postcards they were going to mail, the total came to 5,000!

"They didn't have much money to spend," Linda says, "but what little they did have they wanted to spend on postcards and stamps to share their experience with their families back in Indonesia."

For Paul and Linda Agus, it was one more precious memory added to their lives thanks to Amway. For the rest of us, it's one of many vivid illustrations of the expansive global reach of the Amway opportunity and the common dreams that drive the human experience regardless of country or culture.

Paul and Linda had every reason to help the struggling Indonesians, for their own path to becoming Diamonds had also been a long, hard climb. It usually is for pioneers.

Originally from Indonesia, Paul and Linda learned of the Amway business while living in Australia; Paul's high school friend Robert Angkasa sponsored them. At the beginning, Linda was petrified to talk in front of people, which she says is one reason she had decided to be an accountant. "This business changed me bit by bit," she says. "I *love* talking in front of people now."

The Aguses made it to the Silver Producer level in Australia. They had gained enough confidence in themselves that when Amway opened in Indonesia in July 1992, they decided to sell all their possessions and return to their native land to build their business and spearhead the Network 21 organization's efforts in that country.

"We thought it would be easy, but it was not," Linda remembers. Recalling his headaches—from the lack of adequate materials in the right language to troubles with the local police—Paul echoes Linda's sentiment: "A lot of people believe a new market is going to be easy. But you have a lot of challenges. Fortunately, our dream was bigger than the challenges."

Their dream was interrupted by illness: Linda's father had a heart attack. He was hospitalized for two months without health insurance, draining the family's savings.

The doctor told Linda her father would only survive with open heart surgery, an operation that had to be done in Singapore or Australia.

Linda was beside herself. Treatment was delayed while she and Paul tried to raise the money. They tried to borrow funds from relatives and were turned down. Linda was angry at first, but then realized, "It's not their fault. Why don't *we* have the money? It's *our* fault." Going deeply into debt, they borrowed the money and transported Linda's father to Singapore. He had the operation, but it was too late; he passed away.

In her time of grief, Linda vowed, "This will never happen to my family again." She and Paul poured themselves into their business, building a large Indonesian business and going Diamond. "We paid off our debts in a year."

Linda learned a lesson she conveys to everyone she meets: "Please, do this business *before* you need it."

As Linda focused on the reasons why she and Paul *had* to succeed, Paul reflected on the reasons why they *did* succeed. "Indonesia is growing so fast for us because we have the best uplines in the world," he explained, crediting Indonesian Robert Angkasa, Australians Mitch and Deidre Sala, and Americans Jim and Nancy Dornan, who "created a support system that works everywhere in the world."

AN INTERNATIONAL FAMILY

Think about it. A direct sales business was started by two Dutch-Americans in a basement in Ada, Michigan. They paved the way a dozen years later for a couple from California to create a support system that spread across the Pacific to a couple from Australia, whose dedication and support are revered by Indonesians struggling to help lift themselves and their nation out of poverty.

Amway has inspired the creation of an international family of doers and dreamers whose collective efforts are helping to advance free enterprise and economic progress even in the poorest of countries. It is a family actively enhancing the prospects of world peace.

It is a story that needs to be told.

* * *

Most people outside the business don't know and are surprised to learn that Amway is a global phenomenon, operating in more than 70 countries and territories and deriving a majority of its sales beyond the shores of the United States.

A year ago, you could have counted me among those unaware of this fact about Amway. I was traveling in Australia with American Trucking Associations President Tom Donohue and his wife, Liz—close, personal friends of the Van Andel family—when we spotted a newspaper headline reporting on developments regarding Amway Australia. "Amway's in Australia?" I asked in wonderment. Tom set me straight over dinner that night, but ever since, I have remained intensely curious as to how a business that I had considered so quintessentially American could take root and thrive in diverse cultures and countries.

What is the "new world order"? We have been asking that question since the phrase was coined following the collapse of communism and the end of the Cold War. What will take the place of the communist state, the socialist state, and the welfare state? The spectacular growth of global entrepreneurship, epitomized by Amway, points us to an answer. The flowering of freedom and democracy along with the expansion of communications and technology and the availability of low-cost business plans such as Amway's have set a bountiful table of opportunity for average people around the world.

AMERICA'S GREATEST EXPORT

Some countries' lifeblood export is oil; some export cars, some export diamonds, and some export food. America's most precious export is not a commodity, natural resource, or manufactured product, but an idea: putting free enterprise in the hands of the common man and woman. More than one observer has noted irony in the fact that a company whose name is derived from "American Way" is now gaining wide acceptance in countries whose dogma for decades has been "Yankee Go Home."

It's been an eye-opening experience for Executive Diamond Jim Floor. "There once was a big question in my mind whether Amway could succeed in certain countries," he told me. "But we have since gone into some very underdeveloped nations and found that they relate to the same principles of success that we do here.

"It's amazing how similar dreams and goals are from country to country and culture to culture. Amway is making the world a little smaller, bringing people together and breaking down barriers."

Hiroyuki Hori, a young Japanese "salaryman" who quit his job several years ago to devote his full time to his Amway distributorship, echoed that assessment to a reporter: "There is an American Dream but really no such thing as a Japanese Dream. There is little chance for success here, but with Amway I see people succeeding all the time."

Helping people succeed all over the world has in many ways transformed the company at home. Amway has become an export-driven company. The numbers tell a dramatic story. In 1984, foreign sales accounted for just 15 percent of total revenues. Today, two-thirds of company revenues are derived from foreign sales, and that share is expected to climb to 75 percent by the year 2000.

Just as important, the global arena affords a new generation of Amway leaders a chance to make their own mark on the business. Building on their fathers' basic vision, the DeVos and Van Andel children now have a chance to be pioneers in their own right. The same holds true for Amway distributors and their organizations, which can prospect in any country in which Amway operates, as long as they comply with the laws of those countries.

In a business like Amway, which relies so much on the excitement and energy of the people in it, it is impossible to calculate the importance of having new mountains to climb.

TRADE BARRIERS?
WHAT TRADE BARRIERS?

In a surreal ceremony at the White House in the spring of 1996, President Bill Clinton and a gathering of the nation's top automobile manufacturers celebrated what they thought was an auspicious milestone in the annals of international marketing: the introduction of a car with the steering wheel on the right-hand side for promotion and sale in Japan, where people drive on the "wrong" side of the road. Led by the President, the participants waxed eloquent about America's smart and aggressive determination to succeed in previously "closed" markets—witness the tremendous "innovation" of building a car that was actually suitable for those markets!

In fairness, U.S. carmakers *have* made great strides in recent years to improve both the quality and export marketability of their products. But the image of politicians and executives patting themselves on the backs that day for doing the obvious is illustrative of the lackadaisical pace at which many U.S. companies have approached lucrative foreign markets.

Not so for Amway and thousands of other inventive and entrepreneurial companies. While some complain and play the "blame game," Amway has entered the global marketplace with a vengeance. For example:

- Amway has established operations in more than 70 countries and territories.
- Amway Japan boasts a sales force of some 980,000 distributors, selling an average of $40 of products to every one of Japan's citizens. Revenues have more than doubled in five years.
- While most U.S. companies have shied away from Brazil due to its economic and social instability, Amway entered the market in 1991 and signed up 10,000 distributors in its first three days. Sales increased 1,500 percent in three years.

- Amway of Poland signed up 100,000 eager distributors within months after it opened its doors.
- The company's opening in the Czech Republic was greeted by a mass of 20,000 distributors signing up in the first two weeks.
- A 1993 public offering of stock in Amway Asia Pacific Ltd. raised nearly $150 million to finance the company's expansion into China, with demand for a piece of the action so strong that stock prices rose 59 percent on the first day of trading.

Crown Ambassador Jim Dornan, whose Network 21 organization sponsors and trains distributors in many countries, remarks on the common human desires of people around the world: "Their aspirations are like ours. They want security and independence—to take charge of their lives and improve their future."

GOING GLOBAL: AN OLD "NEW IDEA"

While the pace of global expansion has increased rapidly in the 1990s, Amway has had an international strategy almost from the beginning. It began in Canada in 1962— a stone's throw from Amway's Michigan headquarters. Puerto Rico was next, technically part of the United States but culturally distinct from the mainland.

As outlined by Charles Paul Conn in *The Possible Dream*, these forays beyond America's immediate shores were not considered great leaps into the unknown but natural extensions of existing Amway networks:

The time would inevitably come that an aggressive young company like Amway would choose a target country, one not bordering on the United States, and set out specifically to open it as an Amway market.

The target was Australia and the year was 1970.

More than a quarter-century later, Australia is home to a thriving Amway business and very successful distributors, like Triple Diamonds Mitch and Deidre Sala, whose business not only encompasses Australia and Indonesia but stretches to Portugal, Hungary, Poland, South America, Turkey, and China.

At the beginning, Mitch was in the business for extra income; Deidre tried to keep it at arm's length. But, step by step they became more enthusiastic, and step by step they climbed higher on the ladder of achievement. "Since Diamond, our future has been secure," Mitch says, adding that both he and Deidre were able to leave their other jobs. "When you take financial pressure and a job out of your life, there's not a lot else to worry about."

Deidre adds: "It's wonderful to be free from someone else's schedule. Free to be full-time parents to our three children. We have all the pretty material things, but the freedom is the best."

Australia's 1971 opening was quickly followed by those of England in 1972, Hong Kong in 1973, and what was then West Germany in 1975. Clearly, in the early going, Amway felt the most "at home" in countries with a large English-speaking population or with stable economies and well-defined Western-style business and legal cultures.

The pace of expansion was methodical. The company added 10 new countries to its roster in the 1980s, a number that was equaled in just the first few years of the 1990s.

OPENING PREVIOUSLY LOCKED DOORS

Historic events have been generally friendly to Amway:

- The fall of communism in Eastern Europe and the disintegration of the Soviet Union and its empire
- The discrediting of centrally planned economies and state-owned enterprises and the embrace of privatization and other free market principles
- The rise of democracy, particularly in Latin America and South America
- The proliferation of communications technology, mass media, and affordable world travel, leading to the rise of an America-friendly and Amway-friendly global middle class and an explosion of consumerism

Yet, alongside these welcome developments have come a number of problematic twists and turns. The sudden blast of freedom—however exhilarating—has brought down institutions, shredded the cradle-to-grave security blanket of the welfare state, and, in some cases, torn countries apart. Decades of iron rule by authoritarian rulers and regimes have left newly freed nations with poorly developed legal frameworks, educational systems, and economic institutions. Corruption has filled the vacuum in some places, breeding powerful gangs and organized crime syndicates.

The search for order and security has led many to a tempered nostalgia for the past: Forty percent of voters in the July 1996 presidential election in Russia voted for the Communist candidate. It has also been rough politically for many of the heroes who prompted or presided over the Cold War victory. Mikhail Gorbachev's comeback bid for the presidency of the new Russia he helped create was greeted with derision. Margaret Thatcher, Brian Mulroney, George Bush, and, most recently, Lech Walesa were booted from office.

Trouble spots and terrorist states make the world a dangerous place. Communists cling to power in North Korea, Cuba, China, and Vietnam, with the latter two trying to perform a high-wire act balancing a one-party political dictatorship with a free market economy.

Australia, Spain, and Sweden have all elected more conservative governments. Yet the United Kingdom could be on the verge of turning back the clock to a Labour government. In the United States, we elected a revolutionary Congress to drastically shrink the size and scope of government, then we got mad at them for doing what they said they'd do and what we asked them to do!

What do we make of this? Simply that what will arguably be the most important world event in our lifetimes—the collapse of communism and the rebirth of capitalism—is no fairy tale. Revolutions are never neat and tidy.

Amidst the chaos, Amway has burst on the scene, helping people make sense of it all. The very conditions that have proved so disturbing and unsettling for so many are conditions in which Amway thrives: unbridled, freewheeling entrepreneurship, where individuals and families create their own success, little circles connected to other little circles.

Anyone tempted by a retreat to the order and security of "Big Brother" governments ought to talk to Diamonds James and Ildiko Vagyi.

James fled then-communist Hungary when he was 21 years old and moved to Australia. He arrived with no money, spoke no English, and had few prospects for success. The struggle, even in a new and free homeland, instilled in James a fierce determination and an objective realization "that freedom does not come automatically by living in a free country. Working for a boss was not my definition of the freedom I gave up my home for."

So when introduced to Amway, he worked hard to build the business in Australia; then, when the opportunity presented itself, he moved back to a free Hungary to pursue his dreams and help rebuild his homeland.

One of those whom James met through the Amway business was his future wife, Ildiko. Together, they built huge businesses in Hungary and in Poland. Network 21 meetings organized every few weeks in Budapest commonly draw upwards of 25,000 people.

Years before James made his way from Hungary to Australia, he had a brief taste of the promise and potential of freedom. He visited an uncle in Canada at the age of 13 and was astounded by the contrast between that country and the stark, gloomy existence of Eastern European communism. Back in Hungary, James's teacher announced that James would tell the rest of the class about all the "bad things" he saw in the West. James had another idea. He told the truth instead and got kicked out of school!

Today, the teacher who kicked James Vagyi out of school for telling the truth is an Amway distributor, living the dream of freedom and free enterprise. "And we welcome that person," James says.

EUROPE AND THE AMERICAS

In Europe, the time for celebrating the demise of communism has long since passed. In the words of *Fortune* magazine, "a nervous sobriety has set in across Eastern Europe." No wonder. Within two years of the tearing down of the Iron Curtain, unemployment in the region had reached its highest level since World War II. In a single year—1991—the economy of the region shrank by 7.3 percent.

"But slowly, surely, a new generation of post-communist entrepreneurs is emerging," *Fortune* noted more optimistically, "offering the first tangible signs of life amid the rubble of communism—and posing new opportunities for Western managers seeking a toehold in the region."

Amway not only saw this trend coming—it has pushed it along. It opened an affiliate in Hungary in 1991, enabling exiles like James Vagyi to come home. That was followed by the openings of Poland in 1992 and of the Czech Republic and the Republic of Slovakia in 1994.

George and Dorota Wawrzonek are natives of Poland who now live in New York. They have built a successful Amway business to the Emerald level and now focus much time and energy presenting business seminars back in Poland. "Amway is a perfect opportunity for people in countries that are now embracing capitalism," George has concluded.

After the fall of the Berlin Wall but before German reunification, Amway officials noted the eagerness with which residents from East Germany were streaming over to the West, buying up Amway products and taking them back east to sell. Interestingly, years of experience securing both basic necessities and luxury items through black-market channels have conditioned Eastern bloc consumers well for Amway's neighbor-to-neighbor direct-selling approach. Consumers do not have to be trained to secure alternative and nontraditional sources for products.

Crown Ambassadors Peter and Eva Mueller-Meerkatz of Germany have seized upon such opportunities to further build their already hugely successful business.

Triple Diamonds Hans and Eva Nusshold of Austria are also at the forefront of the enormous expansion of Amway throughout Eastern Europe. Both were ski instructors on a job in Australia when they heard about the Amway business, and they carried their knowledge and determination back to Austria. Today, it is not uncommon for Network 21 meetings in Eastern Europe to be attended by thousands of their downline distributors.

Despite their enormous success, the Nussholds' reflections always come back to family. "The business has helped us become better parents," Eva says. "We want to build a huge business for our two little daughters."

* * *

In Latin and South America, both favorable and unsettling conditions make this region fertile territory for Amway as well. Many major U.S. manufacturing and

service firms have shunned countries in the region. Not
Amway. Years of pent-up consumer demand, rising living
standards, and mass communications have whetted the
appetite of many in the Americas both to consume
Amway products and to build Amway businesses.

Brazil is a case in point. Within three days of Amway
Brazil's 1991 grand opening in São Paulo, 10,000 hopeful
distributors signed up. By the end of three years, 200,000
Brazilians were selling $100 million in health, cosmetic,
and cleaning products, prompting the company to chart
plans for the establishment of a distribution center in the
country.

Mexico is unfortunately and unfairly known to many
Americans as a source of instability and illegal immigrants. In fact, despite political and financial turmoil,
Mexico through it all has remained true to a course of
economic reform.

By the end of the 1980s, Mexico had sold off or shut
down two-thirds of its inefficient state-owned industries.
Maturation of Mexico's trade policies were symbolized
by its new membership in the General Agreement on Tariffs and Trades (GATT). The North American Free Trade
Agreement (NAFTA), despite the attacks of opponents,
has enabled Mexico to emerge from the 1995 peso crisis
in far better shape than when the country emerged from
the debt crisis of the early 1980s. A growing middle class
with increased spending power in this huge market of 80
million consumers helps explain why Amway is so gung
ho on Mexico and has seen steady growth there since
1990. The rewards of helping a great, proud people—part
of the American continent and our good friends and
neighbors—cannot be calculated in profits alone.

Many Americans who trace their roots to the countries of Latin and South America are stepping forward to build businesses among those who hail from similar backgrounds or who remain in their homelands.

Victor Rivera was born an American, but the rural poverty he experienced while growing up in his native Puerto Rico seemed worlds away from the affluence of the United States. Despite little formal education and limited English skills, Victor and his wife, Ivette, have freed themselves from the poverty trap through Amway. Now, as Spanish-speaking Emerald Direct Distributors, the Riveras focus their efforts on lining up distributors throughout Latin and South America.

Galindo Martinez grew up in a small town in the Dominican Republic, one of 15 children sharing a small house with no electricity or running water. A sickly child, Galindo developed a strong inner strength from his earliest years. He was determined to pull himself out of poverty so he could realize his dreams and take care of his family.

At age 18, he moved to the capital city of Santo Domingo and put himself through college. It was there that he met Carmen. Carmen knew poverty even worse than that experienced by Galindo and his family. She had been working since she was seven years old. When a friend presented the Amway Plan to her on a paper napkin, her heart pounded with excitement. This would be the avenue to her dreams!

Galindo and Carmen married, and they built an Amway business in the Dominican Republic that caused their friends to marvel at their success. They even bought a car. When conditions worsened in the country and an opportunity to emigrate to New York presented itself, the Martinezes decided to go and build their business there.

Their dream was deferred: speaking no English and needing to make an immediate living, Galindo got a job as a bakery salesman. Eventually, he and Carmen owned two grocery stores and a wholesale candy business, but their thoughts always returned to Amway.

"I came to New York because of that dream, and I never really gave it up," Galindo has said. "It just took all our time and energy for a while to survive. By 1990, we knew we had to change. The strain of nonstop work was overcoming us both. We turned back to our Amway business."

Once they did, it was blastoff time! Speaking only Spanish, they reached the Executive Diamond level and began fulfilling dream after dream. In addition to their home in New York, they own a home with a swimming pool in Santo Domingo. And they built a beautiful home for Galindo's parents, whom they visit every month.

Amway may be an international business now, one that seamlessly bridges countries, cultures, backgrounds, and languages; but in the midst of spectacular global growth, it is still a business that brings families together.

OH, CANADA!

Meanwhile, Amway Canada is such a close member of the Amway family that, for all practical purposes, it is seen as part of a huge North American domestic market rather than a foreign one. Established in 1962 as a natural extension of the company's Great Lakes roots, Amway Canada is home to some of Amway's legendary distributors, like Jim and Sharon Janz of British Columbia.

Jim and Sharon began their Amway business 32 years ago in their basement apartment when Jim was a low-paid junior high school teacher. They have since attained the Crown Ambassador level and are cited by Amway Corporation as among its most successful North American distributors. "This business is just perfect for the '90s," the Janzes say. "People know they have to make their own security."

Another report from the fertile fields of Canada comes from a distributor "chatting" recently on the Internet:

> I just got back from a function in Cleveland. The Scott and M. J. Michaels organization in the Great Lakes region of Canada and the United States is growing by leaps and bounds. A couple from Michigan has just gone Pearl in their first 60 days from starting in the business. They sponsored 60 people in their first month and already have a leg 20 deep. Go do it!

* * *

Thirty years ago, Helen Huebner and her husband, Bert, of Winnipeg began their Amway business when it became apparent that his salary as a teacher just wasn't enough to support their four children. Helen and Bert built their business the way they lived their lives—as a team.

Fifteen years ago, Bert passed away. Helen has since thrown herself into the business with inexhaustible vigor, nurturing the legacy she and her husband started together so many years ago. As a Double Diamond,

Helen is intent on sponsoring young people in the business just as she has done with her own children.

Growing Pains

While less risky from an investor's point of view, the expansion of Amway into Canada more than 30 years ago was not without its problems and controversies. In 1983, the company paid a fine of $25 million (Canadian dollars) after Canadian officials said the company had not paid customs duties for two decades.

Unhappy as they were at this turn of events, the episode taught the founders some valuable lessons that have come in handy as Amway expands its reach around the globe. In a blunt acknowledgment to the *Detroit Free Press* several years ago, cofounder Rich DeVos said: "We were a honky-tonk company that started with a few people, and before you knew it, we were a $100 million business that missed signing a piece of paper 18 years earlier, which made our life miserable for some years."

Now, the company works closely with host governments when expanding into new countries.

THE ASIAN CENTURY

During the late 1980s, I was a senior advisor to the governor of California, responsible for establishing a plan to market the Golden State's products, investment opportunities, and lifestyle to the booming region of the world known as the Pacific Rim. My duties included establishing California trade offices in Japan and Hong Kong and building networks of contacts in countries from Korea to Australia, from the Philippines to Vietnam.

I learned many important lessons about the markets of Asia, among them:

- It is virtually impossible to overstate the dynamism and growth potential of the Asian market.
- Most Americans remain myopic in their view of the cultures and economies of the Pacific. Particularly on the East Coast, the gaze remains firmly fixed on Europe, where the predominately European-descendant business community feels more at home.
- There is not one single "Asian market"—but many. Yet, all have this in common: business is conducted on the strength of personal, family, and ancestral relationships.
- Despite the cacophony of complaints about trade barriers, it is the lack of understanding and patience, rather than trade barriers, that contributes to U.S. export failures in the region.

In addition, John Naisbitt's *Megatrends Asia* depicts the vastness of the Pacific region with the following facts:

- The number of Asians in poverty has decreased from 400 million to 180 million since the end of World War II, even while the population has increased another 400 million.
- The Asian middle class, not including Japan's, will number between 800 million to 1 billion shortly after the turn of the century, amassing $8 to $10 trillion in spending power.

- Currently, more than 80 million mainland Chinese earn between $10,000 and $40,000 a year. In South Korea, 60 percent of those who describe themselves as middle class make over $60,000 a year. One million families in greater Bangkok, Thailand, earn over $10,000 annually. Many Asians are still poor, but many millions more are consumers with American-style purchasing power and American-style dreams.
- The savings rate in most Asian countries is 30 percent or more, making the region awash in capital for spending and investment.

Naisbitt writes:

[The Asian continent] now accounts for more than half of the world's population. Within five years or less, more than half of these Asian households will be able to buy an array of consumer goods—refrigerators, television sets, washing machines, computers, cosmetics, etc. And as many as a half billion people will be what the West understands as middle class. That market is roughly the size of the United States and Europe combined.

The size of the market is only half of the equation we must consider when evaluating the potential for growing an Amway business or other direct-selling business. Among the Asian "megatrends" delineated by Naisbitt:

- A shift from nation-states to networks
- A shift from an export-led to a consumer-driven economy
- A transformation from male dominance to the emergence of women

As much as any other factor, these three trends explain why Amway in Asia has been such a phenomenal success and why it will continue to provide a gold mine of opportunity for Amway distributors all over the world. Let's look at these three factors in more detail.

From Nation-States to Networks

John Naisbitt further observes:

> If we counted the economic activity of all the overseas Chinese as a country all by itself, it would be outranked only by the United States and Japan.

> The overseas Chinese are a network of networks. This is a new paradigm, a new foundation within the framework of the world's economy.

A network of networks—the same can be said of Amway. While most Amway distributors have deep roots and a deep commitment to both their community and country, the most successful Amway businesses pay precious little attention to geographic boundaries. Crown Ambassador Dexter Yager, for example, does business in almost as many countries as Amway Corporation itself!

Conceptually, the overseas Chinese network that Naisbitt mentions operates in a similar fashion. In this case, family, ancestry, and ethnicity override country of residence when it comes to business contacts and transactions.

Both the Chinese network and Amway provide an interesting snapshot of how the global economy is going to operate in the future, facilitated greatly by developments in communications technology and the ease of foreign travel.

From Export-Led to Consumer-Driven

Good networks are meaningless if the people in them have no money to spend. That's not the case in Asia. A recent front page report in the *Wall Street Journal* sums up what's happening succinctly: "Major U.S. Companies Expand Efforts to Sell to Consumers Abroad," the June 13, 1996, headline reads. "Many no longer consider emerging nations merely sources of cheap labor."

The story chronicles the successful penetration of growing consumer markets by U.S. companies, relating examples such as Citibank credit cards in Thailand and Frito-Lay snack foods in China. Last year, Frito-Lay sold 100 million bags of Cheetos in a single Chinese province!

Many firms are utilizing direct sales as the entrée to the markets. American International Group has signed up 5,000 people in Shanghai alone to sell insurance door to door. Citibank pays each of its credit card salespeople in Thailand on the basis of how many approved applicants they sign up.

This is a new equation. Whereas in the past U.S. companies eyed developing nations in Asia and elsewhere primarily as sites for manufacturing facilities and sources for natural resources, today they view the local populations as the customers for the products themselves—especially as U.S. population and income growth flatten out.

Many of us in Western countries, particularly those of us who have achieved high levels of material affluence with relative ease, are quick to deride the consumerism rampant in Asia. But we should remember that throughout history and throughout the twentieth century, securing a full bowl of rice in these societies has been a daily challenge, even a life-and-death struggle; therefore, achieving the means to obtain home appliances, decent clothes, cars, tickets to the movies, or a dinner out in a restaurant symbolizes something important and profound to many Asians.

Emerald Tonny Supriyanto from Indonesia is a small but proud part of the new Asian spending power. For Tonny, the opportunity to come to the United States and shop for clothes on fashionable and expensive Rodeo Drive in Beverly Hills was a milestone achievement, which he enthusiastically described in a speech to Amway distributors in California.

Growing up poor in a small Indonesian town, "I became a gangster in school," Tonny admitted. It was all tough talk and the swagger of a bully. "I had $25 a month in pocket money. I had no future at all."

Becoming an Amway distributor helped Tonny take responsibility for his own life and for others. "My parents were surprised and proud," he said, "and a lot of downlines who don't listen to their own parents now obey me. I'm acting like a surrogate parent, and I'm changing their lives for the better."

For a new generation of Asians seizing the heretofore unheard-of potential to free themselves and their families from a history of grinding poverty, there's the Rodeo Drive dream, but there's also the dream of helping others, lifting up their country and making their parents both proud and comfortable.

* * *

In the course of preparing a book on business opportunities in Vietnam, I witnessed firsthand the stirrings of the new Asian middle class in that country. The pace of economic change and the growth of consumer demands—indeed, the manner in which consumerism and commercialism has consumed Vietnam's urban populace—is staggering.

In the early 1990s, just as Vietnam was transforming itself from a stagnant, centrally planned economy to one based on market incentives, I stayed at a premier hotel in the heart of Saigon, now called Ho Chi Minh City. At that time, the front desk clerks entered guests' names in a handwritten ledger. Bills were calculated on an abacus. The room had a phone with no dial or keypad; it simply connected you to the front desk and the hotel's two outside lines. Soap and toilet paper from "Products Company No. 3" and a flask of boiled water were the only amenities.

The trip from the airport to the hotel was accomplished in an old Peugeot after some vigorous bargaining (in dollars) with the driver. Ours was one of the only vehicles on the road that was not powered by foot.

One year later, I returned, checking into the same hotel after a ride from the airport in a brand-new, air-conditioned Toyota taxi with a meter (still calculating the fare in dollars). The streets were clogged with new Honda motorcycles. The hotel clerks checked me in on a computer and totaled my bill on a calculator. My room was equipped with a push-button phone with international direct-dial. A vast array of drinks, bottled water, and snacks was available in the mini-bar, and the amenities included international brand-name soaps, shampoos, lotions, and a toothbrush.

I also had the opportunity to visit a number of typical Vietnamese homes. While primitive by Western standards, within the space of several years I watched one typically middle-class home become equipped with a washer/dryer, TV and VCR, cellular phone, and a full complement of personal- and home-care products, including U.S. brands of cosmetics, cleaners, lotions, and shampoos.

As Vietnam increasingly opened its doors to the world, I also saw overseas Vietnamese returning to their homeland with overstuffed suitcases and satchels of consumer goods specifically requested by their consumption-deprived family members. Noting which goods were and are most requested from returnees by their families is one good barometer of current domestic demand. Local Vietnamese ask for cosmetics; high-quality personal products, such as skin creams, vitamins, and baby items; candy and snacks; kitchen products; "name" products indicating the status of affluence. Products "made in the U.S.A." are a plus.

Vietnam, with its strong Chinese influences, mirrors what is happening all around Asia. Would these new legions of middle-class consumers also make good distributors? Let me answer that question with this story:

A family I befriended in Ho Chi Minh City lived in a back alley tenement; but as the family progressed economically, it was time to look for new digs "uptown." Did they want to find a quiet suburb off the beaten track, near a park for the kids, or perhaps a golf course condo for the adults? Not on your life! "We want a place right on a busy street, with our front door opening up onto the sidewalk," my friend told me.

"Why in the world would you want that?" I asked.

"It's too noisy. It's too busy. It's too dirty!"

"So we can sell things," she replied.

By the turn of the century, the Asian middle class will become the most significant consumer force in the world—and most of them look upon selling as a virtue, not something to be looked down upon.

From Male Dominance to the Emergence of Women

"Entrepreneurship is flourishing among women in Asia," writes John Naisbitt. He cites these facts to prove his point:

- One in five management jobs in Hong Kong is held by women.
- The number of female managers in Singapore has nearly tripled in the last decade.
- Five out of six new businesses in Japan are created by women.
- Women have accounted for 25 percent of all business starts in China since 1978.

The Amway business has always been female friendly; Asian business has not—but that is changing fast. Amway's focus on products for personal and family use, combined with the explosion of entrepreneurship and new assertiveness among Asian women, is a perfect marriage and figures to be a long-lasting one.

For Hitomi Yokomizo, the Amway opportunity could not have come at a better time. When this young Japanese woman came to California to study photography, she was sure that all her friends back home would only want to hear about beautiful beaches, Hollywood stars, and Disneyland. What was curious is that they also kept asking her to check out Amway!

It was fortunate that they did and that Hitomi started such a business, because an accident damaged her eyes and forced her to forgo her dream of a career in photography. Amway offered her a way out of the shock and disappointment. Today, Hitomi is at the Emerald level and strongly recommends the business to Asian Americans.

AMWAY'S ASIAN STRATEGY

Since the early days of toil and dreams in the basements of the Van Andel and DeVos family homes, Amway has been a family-owned and family-operated business. The challenge of introducing the Amway product line and business opportunity to the teeming billions in Asia has prompted the company to take at least a piece of its empire public for the first time. Doing so not only has raised cash for the company's expansion into China but has helped establish a market value for the Amway approach to business.

Because the company depends on independent distributors to market its products, the question has long been asked: What is a direct-selling company like Amway really worth? How do you place an accurate value on a company that is primarily relationship-driven? Are we talking about real money or "monopoly" money?

Taking small pieces of Amway public should still those questioning voices.

The company has created two new entities—Amway Japan Ltd. and Amway Asia Pacific (AAP) Ltd.—and established them as distinct companies with stock publicly traded on the New York Stock Exchange. Established market value of the units: an estimated $5.1 billion for Japan and $1.6 billion for Asia Pacific!

In business now for 15 years, Amway's Japan business has a long track record of growth. So, investors were impressed, but not necessarily surprised, when in 1994 Amway Japan Ltd. successfully completed a global secondary stock offering, reducing to just under 85 percent the stock owned or controlled by the founders and their families. Investors in Japan and the United States reacted with equal enthusiasm to the high-growth, low-debt Tokyo-based firm—only the tenth Japanese company to be listed on the New York Stock Exchange.

But it was the establishment and public offering of shares in the Hong Kong–based Amway Asia Pacific, with its plan to enter the China market, that created a buzz of excitement in financial markets in 1993.

"Amway's Asian Unit Is an Instant Hit as Investors Drive Up Price of Stock 59% in First Day of Trading," read the headline in the *Washington Post* on December 16, 1993. Selling off approximately 4 million of 55 million available shares, Amway Corporation raised $142 million from the offering.

Amway in Japan: Breaking Barriers

At first glance, the story of Amway Japan appears typical for Amway—it has success written all over it. Published financial reports on the company paint a picture of financial health:

- As of the end of fiscal year 1995 (August 31, 1995), the company had 980,000 distributors with a renewal rate of 72 percent.
- Gross profits for the year increased 14.5 percent over the prior year's.
- Of the 130 products offered in Japan, the Amway World Plaza collection of apparel and accessories, including 58 newly introduced products, were the hottest sellers.
- Artistry Self-Acting Skin Cream, other skin care products, and the Triple X food supplement are also enjoying brisk sales.
- With land in Japan worth much more than its weight in gold, a further indication of the company's robust health was its purchase last year of two parcels of prime Tokyo real estate for a new headquarters and distribution center.

Success the Amway way—prudent, steady, methodical. But it wasn't easy, especially when dealing face to face with Japan's byzantine distribution system.

For years, experts have tried to reconcile the fact that while Japan's overt trade barriers—tariffs and quotas—were low by global standards, trade deficits remained stubbornly high. In my own trade development work on behalf of California, the number one complaint I heard from frustrated exporters and marketers was that the rigid Japanese distribution system simply froze them out. They could get their products to the *shores* of Japan, but not into the *stores* of Japan.

Start-up Japanese companies and service providers have confronted similar roadblocks. For Japanese consumers, the result has been artificially high consumer prices—the highest in the world.

Fortune's Emily Thorton observed the following:

> Even when the economy was booming, Japan had one glaring problem: a distribution system as labyrinthine as a shogun's palace. Everything a consumer bought—made in Japan or imported . . . had to wend through the books of as many as a half dozen middlemen. Some of them never took possession of the products, but all extracted a toll, creating the world's most exorbitant prices. A bottle of 96 aspirin tablets costs $20, and not just because of the strong yen.

Richard Johnson, president of Amway Japan, explained the challenge this way in a recent interview in *Institutional Investor:*

> It's not so much that the government or society has said foreign products can't be distributed. It's rather that the major manufacturers have created a very disciplined distribution channel and don't permit any outsiders in, be they foreign or domestic.

Johnson cites the beer industry as an illustration of the kind of "discipline" he's talking about:

> Up until a short time ago, Kirin Brewery Co. basically dominated the wholesale network. It was very hard to introduce a new product, regardless of all the advertising a company did, because then bars could only order what their wholesalers would provide. And the wholesalers might say, "If you want a case of Sapporo or Suntory, you've got to take 10 cases of Kirin."

Given that Amway is founded on the notion of bypassing the normal distribution chain wherever it operates, Amway Japan represented nothing less than a direct, frontal assault on the business establishment. "Our start-up was very difficult," Johnson recalls. "We did very little business in the first five years."

Today, the Amway business in Japan is not only thriving, it has spawned an array of imitators, which together are revolutionizing the tastes and practices of Japanese consumers. Other U.S. product manufacturers, confounded for decades by trade and distribution barriers, are now turning to Amway, hoping to have their products included in the company's offerings to distributors and consumers.

What accounts for Amway's ability to overcome roadblocks that have stopped so many others? In addition to the universal appeal of its business opportunity, the company has had three other factors working in its favor:

1. Japanese consumers
2. Japanese dreams
3. Japanese women

New Opportunities in Japan

If you think America has been in the economic doldrums for much of the 1990s, consider Japan. A deep recession, fueled in large part by a bust in land prices, has shaken the Japanese, torn at the carefully woven social fabric, and plunged the country into a national identity crisis. It's easy to see why, considering the significant challenges the society faces: the recession, the aging of the population, the inability of the political system to respond quickly and effectively to problems, and an ill-defined role in the world.

Yet to write off the Japanese as a has-been world power, as John Naisbitt seems to do in *Megatrends Asia*, is unfounded. The economy is now rebounding strongly. The Japanese people are both demanding and making change; they are refusing to put up with that which they once quietly and stoically withstood.

Many consumers are asking, "With money so tight, why should we have to pay the highest prices in the world just so a product can pass through the hands of five or six middlemen to reach us?"

"All the ferment, and the new willingness of Japanese consumers to give American innovations a chance, are creating opportunities for U.S. companies to transplant to Japan successful business strategies from back home," concludes Emily Thorton in *Fortune*.

But dreams as well as tight family budgets also help explain why Amway has taken root in Japan. "Many of the distributors are refugees from the stultifying, hierarchical world of Japanese big business," observed Yumiko Ono in the *Wall Street Journal*. "They want to work for themselves and be paid according to their performance, not according to their seniority. The growing number of people who do marks a big change in Japanese society."

For many Japanese, the 1990s have seen the compact between employers and employees broken. As I discussed in chapter 2, many companies have had to downsize. Employees have wanted something more, too—something more out of their professional lives than working one job at one company, wearing the corporate uniform every day from age 25 to age 60.

That goes double for many Japanese women. Japanese homemakers have long held immense sway over their country's economy—controlling the household money and purchasing decisions, even parceling out allowances to their "salaryman" husbands for their bowls of noodles at lunch and after-work beers and snacks with colleagues.

For all the collective spending power enjoyed and exercised by Japanese housewives, however, it has proved to be a boring, suffocating existence for many. For a brief period, Japanese women experience some freedom: higher education away from home, an international trip to Hawaii and California with schoolmates, a job in a nice office in Tokyo. Then, for most women, comes marriage. One or both spouses leave home in the predawn darkness for the 90-minute train ride to work and return exhausted long after dark, day in and day out. While conditions are changing for working women, the glass ceiling for these women in the corporate world remains a formidable and foreboding barrier.

So it is not surprising that reporter Ono would come across young Japanese couples like the Kakuwas. Mr. Kakuwa quit his job in a machinery business three years ago to join his wife's Amway business. This would have been an unheard-of circumstance in Japanese society a few years ago, and it is still the exception to the norm today.

Another Tokyo distributor, Junichi Ebine, described his motivation for joining Amway this way: "People are starting to wonder what they could do as a single gear in a company. They want to have fun, they want to do something. But they have nothing. When they join Amway, there's something that clicks."

Forbes reporter Gale Eisenstodt assesses Amway's appeal in Japan by observing, "Amway's be-your-own-boss pitch may be greeted cynically in the United States, but in regimented Japan it finds a willing audience, especially among housewives and frustrated salarymen."

Yet Amway's success in Japan is much more than a response to the negative. Amway works because it taps into some of the most positive qualities of Japanese culture as well:

- The importance of one's personal network of family, friends, and associates
- The focus on quality and the demand for superior products
- The commitment to hard work and saving
- An unabashed pride in what one does and the organization to which one has become attached

Amway ranks second only to Coca-Cola as the most successful foreign company in Japan; it has enabled nearly a million Japanese to tap into the very best of their culture while at the same time effectively responding to frustrating conditions around them. The *Wall Street Journal* summarized it neatly and succinctly in the headline of a recent story: "Amway Translates with Ease into Japanese."

CHINA AND THE ASIAN FRONTIER

April 10, 1995: the day Amway began perhaps its most ambitious expansion to date, taking the first steps to bring Amway products and the Amway direct-selling business opportunity to the nearly one-quarter of the earth's population that live in the People's Republic of China.

Guided by the experienced hand of Eva Cheng, Amway Asia Pacific's executive vice president based in Hong Kong, the company has methodically laid the groundwork for its move into China. It began with an inaugural product line consisting of three household cleaners and two dishwashing detergents. A $100 million manufacturing facility established in Guangzhou makes home- and personal-care products. Eight distribution facilities have been established in the southern provinces of Guangdong and Fujian. A strong presence has been launched in Shanghai as well.

There have been some hurdles and headaches, however. As Amway president Dick DeVos told the *Grand Rapids Business Journal:*

> In a country in transition, with an economic model that is evolving, the issues for us are those such as the issue of infrastructure. That country requires a tremendous amount of infrastructure to support an American style of distribution, and we have to work within the support structure. That means limited phone lines and all sorts of infrastructure issues.

So why do it? After all, Amway Asia Pacific has done just fine without China. As Amway's exclusive distributor for the burgeoning markets of Australia, New Zealand, Malaysia, Thailand, Taiwan, Macau, and Hong Kong, AAP enjoyed more than 17 percent growth in fiscal year 1995 over 1994.

A big reason can be summarized in a single Chinese word, *guanxi*, which refers to one's connections. Chinese business and society are built on *guanxi*, and the concept is extremely compatible with Amway's formula of achieving success by building and nurturing a multifaceted network of contacts. Such connections may have come about from sharing a common ancestry, hailing from the same village, attending the same school, working for the same company, or being married to siblings from the same family. Just like all those "crazy circles" drawn by Amway distributors, Chinese look continually for new ways to expand their *guanxi*.

Neither physical boundaries nor long-running political disputes will get in the way. In fact, distributors of a Chinese ethnic background who are in Taiwan and Hong Kong have reacted with such enthusiasm to the prospect of signing up distributors on the Chinese mainland that AAP has detected a discernible drop in new recruits in the Taiwan and Hong Kong markets; 1996 sales in the region, except for Thailand and Malaysia, have lagged as well.

Watching the Chinese expansion sap both corporate and distributor energies and resources was surely anticipated by Amway's leadership; it is one more illustration that creating Amway China will be a long, slow process, but one that will ultimately pay off.

"The first thing that attracts any marketer is the magnitude of China," Dick DeVos has observed. "But the thing that impresses us long term and allows us to maintain a long-term perspective is that it's a very big country, developing and changing very rapidly. Our concern is that we're in a position in the marketplace that will stand us in good stead for the long term. We are going to be operating very carefully."

Alice Kung, on the other hand, sees only opportunity and she sees it right now! As told to the *Far Eastern*

Economic Review, she left her home in America and
returned to her ancestral home in Guangdong to sell
Amway products and sponsor distributors.

Recall our earlier discussion of John Naisbitt's mega-
trend of nation-states to networks. Entrepreneurs like
Alice Kung are living examples of this transition. Within
10 days of her arrival in China, she sold Amway Business
Kits to 60 prospects. "I'm so flooded with these requests
that I don't even have time to call up my own friends
here yet," she told the magazine. "In another six
months, I could be sponsoring 500 to 600 people. . . ."

A GIFT TO CHILDREN

When I directed California's trade development programs, my colleagues and I spent enormous energy trying to decipher a riddle: how to convince the over-
whelming majority of businesses in the state—small
businesses—to add or at least consider an international
dimension to their operations. The "big guys" needed no
prodding, and neither did recent newcomers to California, especially those who left Asian homelands with
their *guanxi* and personal family resources relatively
intact. It was another matter entirely to sway smaller
businesses stuck within their safe, local confines.

In thinking about the importance of adding an international dimension to a business, consider the following:
Amway offers people the opportunity to run an international business out of their den. Distributors can sponsor
distributors in any country where Amway operates, consistent with the laws of those countries; doing so wisely

adds an exciting dimension to business and life. People and their families can create the opportunity to see and experience the world through the eyes of their downline distributors. If they are successful, they will have ample opportunity to travel the world and see for themselves. Can you think of any better way to prepare our children for the global economy of the twenty-first century?

In the case of Executive Diamond Jim Elliott, chairman of the International Networking Association, a strong business focus on opportunities in Latin and South America not only enlarged his family's horizons, it enlarged his family. In the course of conducting their business, one of Jim's sons met, fell in love with, and married a young woman from Argentina. Today, the couple works with Jim to build the international dimension of the family's Amway business.

Crown Ambassadors André and Françoise Blanchard's son, Martin, moved to São Paulo, Brazil, and built an impressively large Amway business in that country. With that mission accomplished, he moved on to Lyons, France, to build the business there.

Crowns Chuck and Jean Strehli go to a different country every month—and then return to their beloved Texas. They have said the international dimension of their business is among its most exciting and rewarding features. "It has allowed us to travel the world as a family averaging a week a month for the past 25 years," Jean says.

Thanks to their Amway business, Mitch and Deidre Sala are also fulfilling "a long-term dream of living in other countries with our children for several months at a time."

American readers, consider this: Surveys cited recently in *USA Today* and the *Washington Post* reveal

some astounding gaps in our children's knowledge about
the world around us:

- One in seven couldn't locate the United States on
  an unmarked map.
- One in four couldn't find the Pacific Ocean.
- Forty-one percent couldn't identify the body of
  water west of South America (the Pacific Ocean, of
  course).
- Fifteen percent thought Brazil was in Africa.

Who knows—the adults may not score much better!

Suppose there was a way you could make money,
build an international business, teach your children
about the world, and prepare them for the global marketplace. There is a way: Amway! Suppose there was a way
for *you* to help bring people together, people who for
centuries have been pulled apart by religious and ethnic
strife? How could this possibly be accomplished with an
"army" made up of distributors and "weapons" consisting of easels, magic markers, and Amway starter kits?

Ask Joe and Mary Logan. Twenty-seven years ago,
Joe was putting in long hours as an engineer in the
Apollo space program in Houston, Texas. "I was helping
to put a man on the moon, but I didn't see too much
future in it." When a friend at Texas Instruments introduced Joe and Mary to Amway, they jumped at it and
reached the Emerald level in 16 months. With a strong
business backing them here, Joe and Mary decided to
move to Mary's native country to build a business there,
so in 1973 they were off to England.

At first, they grappled with a big obstacle: the fact
that some unscrupulous operators there had previously

given direct-selling companies a bad reputation. But they overcame that and built a successful Emerald business in the United Kingdom as well. "We moved back to the United States in 1977, as Emeralds in both countries."

"The key to Amway is the ongoing income you get," Joe told me. "I got in when I was 27, I basically retired from my job when I was 31, and I have been financially independent ever since."

For all the comfort and security the Amway business has brought to the Logans, one magical moment stands out in their minds. "Several of our Diamonds in Northern Ireland organized a meeting and invited us to speak," Joe told me. "The meeting was held in the most bombed hotel in Belfast. And it struck me that we had 500 people in that room, probably divided half and half between Catholics and Protestants. And you know something? That day, in that room, learning about this business, they didn't care.

"This business is magic, bringing people together of vastly different backgrounds and religions, some with centuries of hatred behind them.

"For Mary and me, that was one of our magic moments, and it still sends chills down our spines."

8

A Team Sport

I ought to be mad at Jim Elliott. After all, I was well along in completing a first draft of this book when Jim and I met for dinner in a hotel coffee shop in Southern California.

By the end of the dinner, I realized I had to tear up much of what I had already written and start over.

I had become captivated by the notion that Amway was a business defined almost entirely by the ethic of rugged individualism—the entrepreneur standing alone, self-sufficient and totally independent, living a life of bountiful materialism and splendid isolation—that's the Amway I was trying to depict and was determined to find. It was of course a caricature—a somewhat appealing one and, like most caricatures, containing some elements of truth, but it was a caricature nonetheless.

To be sure, many people in Amway have a lot of the above-mentioned qualities. The dream of taking control of their lives and declaring independence from employers and government is indeed a powerful magnet. But what I was missing was Paul Harvey's proverbial "rest of the story." Jim Elliott set me straight. He opened my eyes to the importance of the *team* in building a successful Amway business. You are indeed in business *for* yourself, he helped me to understand, but you are not in business *by* yourself.

The next morning, one of the successful Diamonds whom Jim had mentored as part of his team told me, "Life is a team sport. So is Amway."

At first, considering his role as chairman and driving force behind the very successful International Networking Association (INA), I half expected to find in Jim Elliott a refugee from the corporate world who was now trying to bring a cookie-cutter approach to a very entrepreneurial business. (It just goes to show that even fervent advocates of capitalism like myself stereotype its practitioners in ways that help perpetuate its negative image.) After talking with Jim, I realized just how wrong I was.

"Helping people is what attracted me to the Amway business," Jim told me. "I got a master's degree from Rutgers in social work and fully intended to pursue a career in The United Way or in a similar organization. I came to realize that this business was the most effective way to help people in meaningful ways.

"Think about it," he continued. "The business builds strong families because it gives parents an effective way to serve as good role models for their kids. It enables children to take care of their parents when they grow old and parents to leave their children a lasting legacy.

"The most important thing Amway does is give you a chance to have a lasting positive impact on other people's lives. You help others reach their dreams and in turn you reach your dreams. This business works because we do it as a *team*."

Jim and his wife, Sharon, recently marked their twenty-fifth year in the Amway business—a business they started not because they wanted to be in business but because they wanted to help people. No social program, welfare scheme, or charity could hold a candle to the power they saw in Amway to measurably better society.

NO LONE RANGERS HERE

Jay Cuccia, a 43-year-old Diamond, once thought he did not need the kind of team behind him that the Elliots had to offer. He planned to do it all on his own. "I took organic chemistry in college and was going to go to medical school to study dentistry," Jay told me. "But I realized that the lifestyle wasn't what I was looking for. I was attracted to the entrepreneurial life, so in the late 1970s I went into the construction business. I married Jan in 1979. She had a real estate license, and I had a contractor's license, so I thought we made a pretty good team."

"Wait a minute, Jay. Wasn't 1979 the year interest rates blew through the roof to over 20 percent?" I asked.

"You got that right," he replied. "It was a terrible time for the housing market, and I just sort of lost my direction and meandered around." Jay fell into a pattern of destructive behavior, including drug abuse. "It almost killed me," he says. "I was literally going down for the third time. I really hit bottom. Then Clarke Broome showed Jan and me the Amway Plan. Within eight months, it had pretty much changed my life. The business had everything I was looking for."

Well, almost. Jay couldn't resist an opportunity to go back into construction. He built a successful vinyl-siding business, hiring employees up and down the state of California. Meanwhile, with Jan, he continued to build the Amway business. He began to notice how many fewer headaches the Amway business brought compared to his construction business, where he was constantly worrying about employees, overhead, contracts, regulations, and lawsuits.

So, at the age of 35, Jay Cuccia left the housing business and never looked back. He has since emerged from that "retirement" only once—to build Jan's dream house!

Jay recognizes that joining a Direct Distributor system may appear to clash with the notion of total self-sufficiency. "Remember, I was self-employed when I came into Amway. It took me a while to accept the idea that I needed someone's help.

"We are rugged individuals within our business. There's no cookie cutter here. But this is a posse deal, not a lone ranger deal."

This former "lone ranger" entrepreneur now understands with great clarity what made Amway work for him: "It's the support group backing you up. Together, we can move a large volume of product, and I can plug into our business people I know from all over the country.

"What a team approach gives you is the gift of encouragement. People I bring into the business tell me, 'I want to be part of a team.' When you have encouraging people around you, you have great teachers—mentors you can really admire."

Jay has found in his team the kind of survival spirit that is usually found only on the battlefield or on a championship sports team. "Except in *our* team, the winning season never ends. It's a lifetime thing."

THE POWER OF HELPING OTHERS

It's no accident that the most successful people in Amway have placed great emphasis on developing and participating in a method to help people like Jay and Jan Cuccia succeed. Each of Amway's major independent business organizations—Dexter Yager's group, Britt Worldwide, Network 21, International Networking Association, International Connection, World Wide Dreambuilders, André and Françoise Blanchard's group in Canada, the Mueller-Meerkatz organization in Germany, and many others—has its own distinctive character and methodology. But each is based on the premise that the individual's journey to economic success and personal development is best accomplished with a team backing him or her up.

"Everyone in the business knows someone who did not make it," Pat Kaufmann, a leader in the International Connection organization, told me. "Through support and training, people learn how to make the Amway business work for them. We try to take people to a different level—not dependence, not simply independence, but interdependence and teamwork."

One of Pat's teammates, Brian Hays, specialized in management development and training programs during his prior work in the corporate world, so these are issues he has studied and considered for a long time. "Some standardization is important, because most people are in the Amway business part time and they need help," he told me. "A group like International Connection can provide distributors with some umbrella concepts and standard materials so that they can more effectively build their Amway businesses."

In Jim Dornan's eyes, it's rapidly expanding markets overseas that have heightened the necessity for a team approach to the Amway business. In 1990, he and his wife, Nancy, founded Network 21, a training and support method for distributors in the United States and Australia. Its mission is to help entrepreneurs effectively expand their network marketing businesses through a program of training, meetings, materials, contacts, and counseling.

Network 21 has since expanded rapidly around the world. The group accounts for a large portion of the Amway business in countries as diverse as China, Indonesia, and Turkey, and it is eagerly laying the groundwork in advance of Amway's planned opening in the Philippines in the spring of 1997.

"I don't believe our success has happened by accident," Jim told me. "Our approach is to take people within a particular culture, train them here, and then send them to the market as a kind of business missionary.

"We have a global vision in Network 21. It's to build a support method that ignores borders and languages."

When you listen to young distributors like Chiffi Osbaldi of Indonesia—who rose from the streets of Jakarta to prosperity in Amway through the strength of their upline support—and you hear the depth of reverence in his voice when he speaks of the Dornans, you can't deny that Jim is well on his way to achieving that vision.

Rex Renfrow underscored the importance of team support in Rich DeVos's book *Compassionate Capitalism:* "You have to make time for others. There are many times I've gone to help others make presentations when I didn't feel like it. I went to help people when most others wouldn't give them the time of day," Rex said.

"Helping people is so important. When you take an interest in a person and look him or her square in the eye and say, 'I'll help you,' it's powerful."

AN INDISPENSABLE INGREDIENT
OF SUCCESS

Over the years, many Amway distributors have been helped immeasurably by learning from the examples of others either through personal experience or through tapes, books, and printed profiles. So it's ironic that some of Amway's harshest critics have singled out these motivational materials for attack. If this were really a legitimate business, they seem to be suggesting, it would have a singular focus on the movement of products and not on the motivation or education of people.

It's a curious view. I doubt any of these critics have questioned the years of exorbitantly expensive education we require of our doctors, lawyers, airline pilots, engineers, or teachers. Why deny and demean the notion that building a successful network marketing business requires a certain degree of training as well?

Dexter Yager, the business genius whom most people credit with pioneering the concept of creating a teachable and duplicable method, never made it to college. Today, his organization, considered the largest in the business, produces educational and motivational materials that teach thousands of people about business and show them a path to success.

Despite his own spectacular success, Dexter still makes time in his own busy life to read books and listen to tapes. Referring to his wife, he says, "Birdie tries to read at least one new book a month. There are personal development books, inspirational books, spiritual books, skill-developing books, success and organizational principles books. After all, we are in business. Why not be successful at it? A doctor has to keep up with scientific research. A lawyer has to know all the new cases coming down. A minister goes on reading the Bible and theology until the day he dies. Why should compassionate capitalists do any less?"

André Blanchard was a high school dropout. Today, he is a "teacher" as well. His family owns a publishing company that offers inspirational and instructional materials to the French-speaking world and many others around the globe.

Books, tapes, and meetings—strictly voluntary components of the new Amway distributor's development as an independent businessperson—are by all accounts an ingredient of success. Comparing what we put into our mind with what we put into our bodies, Rich DeVos says, "One important way to improve your 'diet' is to *listen to tapes and read books.*"

* * *

Also essential to Amway's durability and flexibility has been the close partnership between the corporation and the distributors. "This is the only business I have ever seen that is truly distributor-driven," says Clarke Broome, an Executive Diamond from Northern California. In fact, over the years, Amway's management has worked with its distributor leaders to capitalize on their ingenuity and individuality.

It can sometimes be a tricky balancing act. The distributors are not employees, yet they are using the company's good name. They also know firsthand what sells and what doesn't, because they are closest to the marketplace of both products and people.

To ensure that distributors have a voice heard by the corporation, the Amway Distributors Association (ADA) was formed. Working out of its own offices in Grand Rapids, Michigan, ADA performs the following roles, primarily through a 30-member board:

- Advises and consults with Amway on all aspects of the business, including product development
- Reviews and amends as necessary the distributor's Rules of Conduct

I asked a number of current and past ADA board members whether they really had a significant impact. Was the board a true partner or just corporate window dressing? To a person, they emphatically stated that they believed Amway listens to their voice.

Dan Williams will never forget the time he served a term as ADA board president. "There I was, sitting in a meeting with Rich DeVos on my right and Jay Van Andel on my left," he recalled. "Someone brought a message in for Jay. He leaned over to me and in a quiet whisper told me he had an important call. He asked me if it would be all right if he stepped out of the room for a couple of minutes.

"It wasn't for show. Jay was genuinely asking me for permission. That demonstrated great respect for me but more important for our board and for all distributors. I have never forgotten it."

THE HEART OF THE BUSINESS

From top to bottom, Amway is a team sport. For Clarke and Diana Broome, the friends and family that make up their team truly define the heart of Amway for them. Clarke grew up in a single-parent family in Sacramento, California, his father having died at a young age. His mother struggled to raise six children on her own. Clarke worked hard, too, so that he wouldn't have to ask her for money.

Diana grew up in a broken home. By age 14, she was living on her own in Southern California, hanging out with a bad crowd and abusing drugs and alcohol. At age 20, she decided it was a road leading to nowhere, so she hit the road to Sacramento. There, she met Clarke, and they later married.

Clarke followed in his mother's footsteps and entered the real estate business. He did so well that he took the plunge and opened his own office. When the real estate boom in California turned into a bust, so did the Broome family finances.

"We owed a lot of money," Clarke remembers. "We were both working constantly, and yet we were getting further behind." Deeply in debt and feeling beaten, Diana wondered whether their family could last. "When we were introduced to the Amway business, I had given up on our marriage," she says.

"We worked long hours, and yet we were hopelessly in debt. All I wanted was a husband and a healthy family who spent time together. We weren't going to ever get that with the road we were on."

Friends advised the Broomes to declare bankruptcy. Clarke would hear none of it. They sold their home and moved into a dark, cramped rental while they built their Amway business and paid off every debt.

Today, Executive Diamonds Clarke and Diana Broome have a beautiful home that is occupied by a happy and united family. Yet the material blessings the business has brought them pale next to the team of friends and family that is assembled around them.

"What we really treasure is the hardest thing to explain to prospects—the real heart of the Amway business," Clarke says. "Each day, I work together with Diana, our kids, and many wonderful friends in the business. We're particularly proud that our organization works so hard to raise money for Easter Seals. It makes us feel really good just to be part of this group."

That's the heart of the business—friends and family. As Dexter Yager says, "Love is the glue that holds this business together." Maybe the Amway experience is the modern way to bring back the neighborliness and concern that people felt for each other in our rural days, when we needed each other to bring in the crops. Maybe it's a way to create the "global village," remembering all the while that each person matters. Whatever it is, one thing is certain. This delicate balance between individuality and interdependence is working every day in the lives of millions of people!

9

Virtual Business— Real Money

The Americans have need of the telephone, but we do not.
We have plenty of messenger boys.
—Chief of the British Post Office, 1876

Brian and Marguerite Hays run their international Amway business out of their home in northwest Illinois. Their staff totals one-half: a part-time secretary.

Jerry and Cherry Meadows operate their Triple Diamond distributorship from their farmhouse in the beautiful hill country of Tennessee.

Brad and Cheryl Biegert built a stately Victorian farmhouse in rural Idaho and run their hugely successful Amway business from there.

Diamonds Steve and Shanna Im live in New York but have enlisted, motivated, and trained many distributors in their native country of Korea on the other side of the world.

Amway has always been a flexible business—a business that allows its practitioners to operate with little or no overhead or inventory according to their own schedule and lifestyle. The Amway opportunity, teamed up with accessible, user-friendly communications and information technology, makes a perfect marriage. More than ever before, it doesn't matter where you live or where you come from, whether you are disabled, or which language you speak—your territory is now the world.

You might call it your virtual business: an office without walls; a warehouse without inventory; a company without a workforce; an asset without capital. All that's left is income!

Sound like science fiction fantasy? It's reality. During a meeting I attended recently with Dr. Brenda Dietrick, a senior executive at IBM, she observed that it is indeed possible today to build and run a multinational business from a 12-by-12-foot room with a phone, a computer, a printer, and a modem. The biggest bookstore in the world, Dr. Dietrick notes, is not really a store at all. It's a virtual bookstore on a Web site on the Internet that does greater sales volume than any of Barnes & Noble's stores—with absolutely no physical inventory!

The "guy running a business from his garage" is the driving engine in today's economy, Dr. Dietrick observes. What empowers these entrepreneurs is the speed with which new communications technologies are made available to the average person. It is technology that is becoming ever more complex in what it can do while at the same time becoming simpler to use and cheaper to buy.

The capacity of the microprocessor is doubling at a rate of every 15 to 18 months and will continue to do so for the foreseeable future, says Dr. Dietrick. She illustrates the impact of this development by recalling that just 10 years ago she attempted to perform a particularly complex function on the largest mainframe computer

IBM had to offer—the kind of computer that used to fill an entire room—and "brought it to its knees"; today, she marvels, she could do the same function successfully and with ease on a "think pad" at her desk!

In the course of my own work in the trucking industry, I have witnessed the dramatic impact technology is having on that business as well. Trucking is not traditionally thought of as a modernistic industry, but one leading trucking executive believes that thanks to technology the future of the business is going to rest "with the man or woman in the cab with a laptop and a cell phone. With those tools and their own rig, they can own a trucking company."

Increasingly, trucks are becoming "rolling warehouses on wheels," as shippers and manufacturers squeeze inefficient steps out of the supply chain. This would not be possible without the development of more reliable equipment and sophisticated technologies to schedule deliveries and track the movement of freight. In fact, in the coming years, bar coding on shipments of goods and satellite tracking of a truck's location will become the norm, as traditional carriers transform themselves into full-service logistics and transportation services companies.

FREEDOM THROUGH TECHNOLOGY

Some wonder whether Amway and the ascension of relatively inexpensive and easy-to-use communications technology are compatible or contradictory. After all, Amway is all about relationships. It's a people business that demands the kind of personal contact that technology simply can't replace.

No doubt technology is challenging and changing Amway, just as it is challenging and changing all of us. Far from making Amway obsolete, however, the explosion of information and communications technology is propelling Amway and the direct-selling industry to unprecedented heights.

Why? Because those technologies have empowered individuals and will continue to do so. They are the tools of independence. You can do things now that you could never before do for yourself. You can build that virtual business and make money, freeing yourself from dependence on government or corporations.

A recent article in *Success* magazine sums up the marriage of entrepreneurship and technology this way:

> Some would say [multilevel marketing] is creating a whole new marketplace "outside the box" of TV advertising, storefronts, inventory, and middlemen and has the power to render the conventional retail world obsolete. That power arises from the union of modern technology— computerized record keeping and telecommunications— with the ancient art of schmoozing.

This "union" has served as a catalyst for Amway and the entire direct-selling industry. Neil Offen, president of the Washington, D.C.–based Direct Selling Association (DSA), spelled out the growing global reach of direct selling, spurred by the growing ease with which individuals in the business can expand their customer and downline distributor networks. In the U.S. alone, more than 7.2 million Americans participate in direct-selling businesses, generating annual sales of nearly $18 billion. Around the world, an estimated 20 million work in the industry—not including those in China.

Richard Poe, a leading authority on network marketing, is so confident that technology and direct selling make a good combination that he sees it bringing on a whole new era, which he calls "Wave 3."

In his bestselling book *Wave 3: The New Era in Network Marketing*, he portrays Jay Van Andel and Rich DeVos as pioneers who revolutionized an approach to selling and to business that can soar to new heights with technology. Furthermore, Poe sees technology as increasing the retention rate of distributors by rescuing the borderline cases from failure and turning them into success stories: "The most advanced network marketing companies today stress simplicity above all. They use computers, management systems, and cutting-edge telecommunications to make life as easy as possible for the average distributor."

The list of new technologies employed by successful network marketing companies just keeps on growing, Poe reports:

Three-way calling, teleconferences, and "dropshipping"— the use of computerized, automated fulfillment systems— have become standard tools for today's network marketer. Fax broadcasting and voice-mail systems now let distributors deliver instructions direct to every person in their downlines. PCs print out envelope labels for mailing lists with thousands of names. Do you want to go global? Wave 3 companies take care of all the customs, taxes, currency conversion, and other hassles of international business. You just go in and make money.

John Fogg, editor of *Upline,* pinpoints the role technology can and should play in building your direct-selling business when he observes: "All of the tools and technology free you up to focus on that one most intangible part of this business, which is relationships with people. Your job is to develop your people and support them in building their business."

What about the customer and distributor networks that Amway businesses work so hard to build and nurture? Will they be undercut by hard-to-control Internet marketing? It's interesting to note that the Amway Distributors Association recently amended the Rules of Conduct to prohibit distributor advertising and selling of Amway products on the Internet. Amway allows only local advertising, and it considers the Internet to be a retail establishment. Amway products are not sold at retail outlets—real ones or virtual ones.

Despite its prohibition of direct marketing on the Internet, Amway is moving fast to provide a technological infrastructure that can help the individual distributor build his or her business and provide better and faster customer service. Distributors may access automated voice reports on the status of their accounts and orders. Customers ordering products from the Personal Shoppers Catalog may do so by calling or faxing a centralized number—and the distributor receives PV and BV credit for the sale!

In 1995, the company market-tested its first catalog on CD-ROM, which enables distributors to electronically order more than 1,000 products and services on behalf of their customers. "We see multimedia technology as an excellent way to communicate detailed product information, making our distributors more productive and successful," an Amway official said. The CD-ROM catalog "offers us the ability to bring products to life by incorporating text, graphics, video, and sound. More important, their interface design makes the catalog easy to use—even for someone new to computers."

Helping the distributor sell products is but one way technology can be used to breed success in Amway; even greater is the impact on the training and motivation of Amway distributors. Major Amway support systems such as Network 21, International Networking Association, International Dreambuilders, International Connection, the Dexter Yager group, World Wide Dreambuilders, Britt Worldwide, and others, are all utilizing the latest methods and technologies to duplicate their successful training and motivational methods all around the world.

ON THEIR OWN TERMS

Can a business built around personal relationships thrive in the sometimes impersonal world of exploding technology? Amway distributors are today harnessing that technology in remarkable ways. They're expanding the geographical reach of their networks. They're doing a more effective job training and motivating their downlines. They're reaching into all corners of the world with remarkable speed and efficiency, giving tens of thousands an opportunity for success. They're doing all this from their basements and dens with their families by their side, living their lives on their own terms.

10

A Conversation
with Skeptics

People have all kinds of excuses. Some say they're too
old. Others say they're too young. Some claim to have
too much education. Others say they don't have enough.
We believe Amway will work for anyone who's willing to
persist.

—Amway Executive Diamond Distributors
Billy and Peggy Florence

In one way, shape, or form I have dealt with the news media throughout my professional life. So I know all about cynicism, skepticism, and pessimism. These, after all, are the tools of the media trade.

Having worked for politicians bent on projecting a particular positive image through the media, I have witnessed and been involved in that intricate, ritualistic dance between press and politician. Politicians spin their messages and fully expect to have them picked apart by the press, so they try to come up with ever more clever ways to project themselves through the media. It's a "blue smoke and mirrors" game.

The Amway distributors I talked to find it hard to conceive how anyone could amuse themselves in such a game. They're frustrated and hurt by the criticism of their business and, with an earnestness bordering on wide-eyed innocence, eagerly addressed the negatives at every opportunity in our conversations.

There are, in fact, many reasons why people don't get involved with Amway—or do and then drop out. Over the years, there has been a lively discussion among current and former Amway distributors as well as among analysts and critics of network marketing as to who is to blame for those who don't succeed.

That debate is overly simplistic. If you've ever been in a management position and have had to make hiring (and firing) decisions, I'm sure you'll agree that sometimes an unsuccessful hire is no one's fault—not the company's and not the employee's. The right fit just wasn't there.

Amway may not be right for everyone. If your personal priorities and circumstances are such that you cannot devote enough time to building your Amway or other direct sales business, then you will not succeed. That doesn't mean you got a raw deal from Amway—nor does it mean you are an inferior person! It simply means that your priorities have changed.

Information is easy to come by in this day and age—everyone's got a posture and an opinion. Yet, serious people trying to make serious decisions about the economic future of their families need hard-nosed intelligence and a vigorous exchange of views. Let's subject Amway to such an exchange.

Is Amway a Pyramid Scheme?

I've indicated earlier that some of the most negative views I have confronted about Amway have come from my own professional peers as I told them about this book. I recall in particular a conversation with one friend who reacted to my topic bluntly: "Amway—that's a pyramid."

I decided to play dumb. "Oh, really? What's a pyramid?" I asked.

"Well, it's, um, I mean, it's . . . I don't really know, I just know I heard that it's a phony business and people are always ripped off."

I suspect many others passing this judgment don't really know what a pyramid scheme is either. They've only heard it's bad and that Amway is one of them. With much clucking of the tongue they condemn Amway and other network marketing approaches as little more than glorified chain letters dressed up as legitimate businesses.

Here are the facts:

While the law is subject to differing interpretations, a pyramid scheme is generally seen as occurring when a business is built almost exclusively on paying people to sign up distributors. New recruits are required to buy major quantities of a product up front (an illegal practice called frontloading), with no opportunity to return for a refund. Little or no attention is paid to moving products to the consumer market. Essentially, participants feed off each other, with the big fish consuming the resources and energies of the smaller fish.

Amway, and with it the entire direct-selling industry, faced a day of reckoning on this score in 1979. The Federal

Trade Commission ruled that Amway was a legitimate business and not a pyramid.

Even though successful Amway distributors devote considerable portions of their time to the prospecting and recruiting of downline distributors, the company has passed muster because the bedrock of its business is the sale of real products to real consumers. Far from the proverbial snake swallowing its own tail, Amway is a global manufacturing, distribution, and marketing company, making, shipping, and selling products all over the world. The company has scrupulously avoided any hint of frontloading. The only investment required on the part of new recruits is the Amway Sales and Product Kit, which costs about $135.

Another litmus test of possible illegal "pyramid" activity is the payment of fees simply for signing people up as distributors. Amway has never done that.

Just the fact that the question has been asked and the FTC has had to rule has been enough to scare off some in today's guilt-by-innuendo climate. If Amway is so squeaky clean, why did the issue even come up? Why has it been so difficult for the company to shake off this charge?

Richard Poe, author of *Wave 3: The New Era in Network Marketing* (Prima), offers the best response and draws an insightful parallel in the process:

> New ideas are always attacked and rejected at first. In its early days, franchising endured similar abuse from the press and from the corporate world, and for almost identical reasons. . . .

The media attacked like hungry barracuda. Exposés featured destitute families who'd lost their life savings through franchising schemes. Attorneys general in state after state condemned the new marketing method. Some congressmen actually tried to outlaw franchising entirely.

How quickly things change! Today, franchises account for 35 percent of all retail sales in the United States.

Amway is no longer a new, untested idea. But its impact is growing geometrically by the day. Other businesses and marketing approaches have competitive reasons for wanting to knock Amway out of the box. Many elements of the established order, including government regulators, big government advocates, and some social activists, aren't really crazy about the notion of millions of independent citizens thinking and doing for themselves.

Still others are negative about Amway because they're negative about their own lives. They're trapped in a rut. They see no way out. Disparaging those who found a way out is necessary to justify their own inability to act. So they raise doubts, cast aspersions, question motives, throw roadblocks across the path of entrepreneurship: "Don't strike out on your own. You won't succeed. The plan is rigged. Get a real job!" they seem to be saying.

The words of Amway Crown Ambassador Sharyn Webb, talking about the Amway business and about life, are worth heeding: "The only fatal mistake you can make is to quit."

I'm Too Good for Amway

Although it enjoys a rich and proud tradition in many cultures, selling is still frowned on by many. This attitude about selling is often seen in people who have a good-sounding job title but a modest income. Indeed, in the course of preparing this book, I confronted a great deal of "attitude" about Amway. I did observe, however, that the most vocal critics were those who have traded opportunity for security in their careers. As a former city manager and now Crown Ambassador Bill Britt likes to say, "I used to have status. I looked good, I smelled good, but I was broke."

For some so-called yuppies, building an Amway business simply doesn't jive with their carefully cultivated self-image as world-wise, white-collar professionals. They want title, rank, and status, even if they have to sacrifice their freedom in the process. They seek the identity that comes from being able to say, "I'm an executive with a big-name company," "I'm a lawyer for such-and-such law firm," "I work for Senator so-and-so." These same people may criticize some Amway distributors for openly setting material goals to wear fine fashions, enjoy cuisines from all over the world, travel first class, buy expensive cars and boats—but most of them crave and want the very same things without admitting it.

There is no question that the idea of being involved in selling on any level deters many people from breaking out of their self-imposed limitations. No such soul-searching was necessary for Rich DeVos, as he wrote in his book *Believe!*:

My own particular "thing" has always been salesmanship. I have been involved in sales all my life, and I am
always amazed to see how many people look down their
noses at salesmanship as a worthy occupation. . . .
I've had people say to me before, "Oh, Amway. You guys
are in that direct-selling deal." My answer: Sure we are!
We are in the personal-service business. We happen to
think that personal service beats making the customer
stand in line. We don't apologize for it.

Have feelings of condescension colored *your* views
about sales generally and Amway specifically? They have
with me.

As I acknowledged at the outset, I had a serious
hang-up about selling. The most difficult period in my
professional life was when I attempted to transition from
the role of a high-ranking government official to operating a consultancy in which I had to sell my professional
services. After years of having the high and mighty
knock on *my* door, suddenly I had to knock on theirs—
without title, without status, without influence. In less
than a year, I beat a hasty retreat back to a politically
appointed office. I blamed a lot of people and circumstances for my failure. It was only later that I realized
that the biggest contributor to it was *my* attitude. I was
simply too embarrassed to sell my wares to my contacts
and associates. I was afraid of rejection. It was beneath
me. Today, I wonder whether I would have succeeded in
my consulting business had I first been actively involved
with the Amway business. I think I know the answer.

Status can cut both ways. Today, Rich DeVos and his
family own the Orlando Magic basketball team. Bill Britt

owns a plaza in North Carolina bearing his name, and Crown Ambassador Dexter Yager received an honorary doctorate from Southwest Baptist College. But there is another, quieter kind of status: the one that comes from working from home without a boss, picking up your kids from school in the middle of the afternoon, and being able to send your parents on an all-expenses-paid trip to Hawaii. That's the kind of status that is enjoyed by many people who are quietly building thriving Amway businesses—perhaps even in your town.

Richard Poe conjures up a future not too long from now:

> You're the last person in America who refuses to become a network marketer. All your neighbors are doing it. All your friends, relatives, and professional colleagues. But not you. . . .
>
> "We'll never give in. We'll never be network marketers. Never!"
>
> But deep down inside, you know it's only a matter of time.

I Don't Want to Sell Soap

It amazes me that to this day, those who know little about Amway and have never bothered to find out more have the misconception that Amway distributors are a bunch of soap salespeople.

The company's original product, L.O.C. Multi-Purpose Cleaner, is still a big seller. But a successful Amway distributor today runs a virtual department store without walls. Goods and services whose diversity boggles the

imagination are available for personal use and for sale—
all told, some 6,500 products from over 1,200 different
manufacturers.

There are hundreds of Amway-brand products, most
of them manufactured at the company's own facilities
and always with an eye toward environmentally considerate processes and packaging. These include products
for the home and for personal use, Artistry cosmetics
and Nutrilite food supplements, and the Amway Water
Treatment System. Even books and CD-ROMs to educate
your child are now available. Then there is the Amway
catalog collection, which offers brand-name home appliances, office supplies, and health and fitness products,
as well as clothing and bulk food. You can even have
aged Midwestern steaks flown fresh to your home!

Perhaps the most noteworthy new development is
the range of *services* Amway distributors now provide
customers, such as MCI long-distance calling plans, VISA
credit card memberships, voice mail, travel planning,
and automobile emergency roadside assistance.

The expansion of Amway into services as well as catalog offerings is significant for several reasons:

- A broader range of products and services means a
  distributor can be a full-service provider to his or
  her customers.
- Distributors receive distributor discounts on a
  much greater array of life's necessities and luxuries.
- Expansion of product and service line increases the
  pool of distributor prospects. For example, an individual working in a bank or phone company, who
  may have been unable to muster the necessary

motivation to sell Artistry cosmetics or Nutrilite food supplements, might become very excited about selling VISA credit cards or MCI long-distance-calling subscriptions.

- The fact that Amway is successfully teaming up with some of America's most respected companies is proof positive of a growing recognition by those companies that direct selling *is the wave of the future.*

People Don't Really Get a Decent Return on Their Time and Investment—Except the Big Guys

There are those who complain they were not able to make a meaningful income from direct selling. Some blame the company. Some blame themselves. Amway is neither a fast-buck routine nor a get-rich-quick scheme—and it has never claimed to be.

Corporate materials spelling out the basic elements of the Amway plan are very up front about who makes it in the business and to what extent. It is true that most Amway distributors do not grow their business to any significant degree of income. Given the low entry fee, one wonders how many of those who purchase their kits approach their involvement in Amway as a serious business opportunity as opposed to a hobby to be dabbled with or an opportunity to purchase products at a discount. There is nothing wrong with joining the Amway business if you want only to achieve smaller goals. And there are always those who do try to one degree or another but do not succeed. That is a fact of life in any endeavor.

Yet, every month, the company's magazine, *Amagram*, identifies hundreds of distributors who have attained levels of Direct Distributor and above—categories in which business volume is achieved.

As I look at the pictures of the new Direct Distributors in the *Amagram*, I try to see what they have in common. Is it their professions or their background? But I fail to see any common denominators. Here are singles and couples. Faces in all the beautiful colors of humanity. Professions? They include doctors, lawyers, teachers, factory workers, corporate executives, government employees, farmers, computer programmers, and on and on. Why do these people succeed while others have not? Perhaps it's because they have set a goal, they have found the inner will to succeed, and they have found a way to overcome their fear of rejection.

So is it worth it? I can't answer that question for you. As I discuss in chapter 6, that's going to depend on how *you* measure success. Not all the value of this business can be calculated in dollars and cents—a great deal of personal growth comes with building an Amway business. As a speechwriter who has heard many government and corporate leaders speak, I am struck by the leadership and speaking skills I have observed in the speeches of most Amway people. Many profess to have been extremely shy of the microphone but now appear clearly at ease, standing in front of hundreds or even thousands of people. Most are better speakers than many of the professional leaders I have heard over the years.

This personal transformation is exemplified by Crown Ambassador Dan Williams, who has suffered all his life from a stutter. He overcame his impediment out of his sheer desire to build his Amway business. Today, he is renowned as one of the most entertaining speakers in Amway. How do you measure the value of that in dollars and cents?

When I was a college student, I earned a couple hundred dollars a month bussing tables in the dining hall to help pay for books and tuition. In retrospect, I would have been much better off building an Amway business, even if I hadn't earned a penny more, because at the same time I would have been learning the fundamentals of operating my own business—skills more valuable to me in the long run than wiping tables.

Let's say you're half of a working couple, and your partner is caught 40 hours a week in a job that's unbearable. You're pulling in $30,000 a year but pay thousands a year for child care you don't really trust. Suppose you make the time to build an Amway business. Sure, you make some sacrifices along the way. But now, you're working from home. You're there for your kids. You're not spending a fortune on child care. You're meeting new people and learning a lot. And, unlike your old job where in 10 years you *might* be earning marginally more, you have the *opportunity* for real growth.

Or perhaps you are a doctor working for one of the big managed-care companies. You remember how much you enjoyed running your own practice, but now you are just an employee and not all that well paid anymore. You long for an early retirement but can't afford it. You start building an Amway business that allows you the opportunity to replace part or all of your income. Impossible, you say? Orthopedic surgeon and Diamond Direct Distributor Clayton Overton is planning to retire early in order to offer his medical expertise to needy patients in Africa. Dreams can and do come true!

Each of us has to cross-check our individual circumstances and priorities against the chances of success in Amway and make a personal evaluation as to its worth. But the charge repeated by some that the chances of making a substantial income from Amway are remote is, quite simply, a bum rap.

One Amway distributor put it this way: "The Amway Marketing Plan works and works well. Many people no longer have to work for anyone else; and lots of people, including myself, have developed substantial incomes. Like so many other things in life, if you stick it out long enough you *will* succeed."

I'll Never Get to the Point Where I Can Quit My Job and Become Financially Independent, So Why Bother?

If you define success only in terms of replacing your full-time income, you have a limited vision of what can happen when you combine extra income with some personal "fiscal responsibility."

For example, if you make $1,000 a month and invest only $500 of it in a conservative mutual fund (yes, Amway even has one of those) for 20 years, you will be worth hundreds of thousand of dollars, based on the average historical performance of the stock market. Do it for 30 years, and you could become a millionaire! If you use sound principles, you can turn your part-time Amway income into a gold mine without ever becoming a "success."

What could you do with such a nest egg? Would you:

- Retire at 55 instead of 65?
- Do the traveling you never had a chance to do?
- Live in the home of your choice?
- Ensure your kids' or grandkids' college education?

You may choose instead to spend your extra $1,000 a month now for things such as private-school tuition for your children or a better health care plan. Maybe your spouse can now work 10 hours less a week in the office and spend it at home with the kids. These represent forms of "independence" too. Or perhaps next year you'll lose your job. Thank goodness you'd still have your Amway income to count on, as well as an existing business infrastructure to grow and expand until you get rehired.

Independence: it's all about options.

I'll Be Pressured to Spend Money on Books, Tapes, and Rallies

Amway is a remarkably cheap way to get into business. The only initial expense is a business starter kit (the Amway Business Kit), which is sold to the new distributor by his or her sponsor for about $135.

Succeeding is another matter. Most of us value education highly. We'll sacrifice, go deeply into debt, or expend our life savings in pursuit of it for ourselves and our children. So why should critics shake their heads and criticize the notion of spending a relatively few dollars for the training and motivational guidance needed to succeed in Amway?

How much education is too much? Where is the line drawn between the legitimate needs of new distributors to learn from the successes and mistakes of those who came before them—and the need to stay motivated—and what amounts to excessive pressure to purchase materials?

The Amway Sales and Marketing Plan states it plainly: "As your business begins to grow, you may want to acquire training aids. You may also want to attend motivational and business-building meetings. These are optional, and the decision is up to you."

I offer this personal observation: In the course of my own effort to fully understand this business, I discovered that as good as the business materials offered by Amway Corporation are, I didn't really comprehend the scope of the opportunity or levels of achievement available *until* I started listening to speeches and tapes of successful distributors.

Amway Corporation May Play Fair, but Some of the Distributors Are Another Story

Amway has a strict Rules of Conduct that all distributors agree to follow. Failure to do so could lead to actions, and even termination, against that distributor by Amway.

A more relevant issue concerns the reputation of the direct-selling or multilevel marketing industry as a whole. Unfortunately, there are unscrupulous operators out there whose dishonesty washes over reputable companies in terms of press attention and public perception. Not all direct-selling companies hold the same high standards as Amway. That's unfortunate, especially given the extent to which the industry's best companies have pledged to police themselves through the auspices of the Direct Selling Association (DSA) in Washington, D.C.

A good way to check whether a particular company enjoys the kind of reputation with which you would want to be associated is to contact the DSA (telephone 202-293-5760 or fax 202-463-4569). President Neil Offen and his staff serve as both advocates for the industry and tough guardians of its reputation. Signing and abiding by the DSA Code of Ethics is mandatory for member companies.

Amway plays a key role in the DSA. In 1997, Amway chairman Dick DeVos is slated to serve as the DSA's chairman.

I'm Single, and Amway's into Family Values Big Time

There's no question the entire Amway organization— from founders to distributors—is imbued with a special devotion to family. At the 1996 North American Annual Convention, cofounders Jay Van Andel and Rich DeVos issued the "Four Fundamentals," which they believe form the basis for a meaningful life. "Family" was one of them. "The family is our primary social structure, providing love and nurturing, heritage and legacy," they have written. "The family provides us with a consistent set of values and a framework for growth and the ability to thrive as individuals."

The married couple is a natural fit for Amway for practical reasons as well. Many couples have built their businesses so that one spouse continues to work in a salaried job, freeing up the other to grow their Amway distributorship. But it is a mistake to say therefore that Amway is unfriendly to single people or that it does not tolerate diversity. Distributors come from vastly different circumstances, occupations, lifestyles, racial and ethnic groups, and nationalities.

Far from condemning the single person, his or her group will eagerly assume the role of a "surrogate" family, providing the love and support the individual may not find elsewhere.

I Don't Want to Be a Part of Amway's Political and Religious Agenda

The Amway Corporation and the Van Andel and DeVos families exercise their civic duties as Americans and participate fully in the political life of the nation. Given their unabashed devotion to the free enterprise system, they naturally support candidates and causes that promote that system.

The difference between Amway's political activism and that of other corporations is that it's not afraid to take a stand. Most big companies spend so much time straddling the fence that they must have severe cases of straddle sores! It is not uncommon for these big companies to make handsome contributions to each of the opposing candidates in a particular race.

Amway's leaders have never tried to mask their political beliefs or water them down; neither has the company ever demanded that distributors or employees march in step with them politically. Contrast that to the big unions' practice of taking mandatory dues payments out of workers' checks to spend on behalf of pro-union candidates, whether the workers support those candidates or not. Nothing like that could or does happen in Amway.

Rich DeVos, for one, is equally up front about the role of religion in his life—but he also draws an important distinction when it comes to the Amway business. "Occasionally people ask me, 'Is Amway a Christian organization?'" he wrote in *Believe!* "I always answer that it certainly is not. . . . I refuse to use the machinery of the Amway Corporation to foist my private convictions on others, and conversely, I do not use the Gospel to promote my business."

11

You Are Not Alone

Compassionate capitalism is a lifelong adventure. No one can tell you where or how you should begin. Just remember that one small act of caring is a beginning. And in that small act—whatever it is—you will be rewarded, and that reward will inspire you to go on to do bigger and better things. Compassion is contagious. Once you have begun, your life will be changed forever.
—Rich DeVos

It happened too much to be a coincidence; it happened too often to be scripted. I asked everyone I talked to in Amway what the business meant to them. What did it do for their lives? What were the greatest rewards reaped for their efforts?

There was broad diversity in the answers, all except for this common theme: the greatest reward in this business is the opportunity to help other people.

When I first started hearing the refrain that people were in Amway to help other people, I was frankly suspicious. I had worked for many years in the political and corporate worlds, and I was cynical about efforts to coat the pursuit of both power and profits in the clothing of charity. At times I felt like saying to the Amway folks,

181

"It's okay. You shouldn't be ashamed by the fact that you're making money. You don't have to cover it up with the veneer of altruism."

It was only later that I came to realize that my suspicion was a product of my failure to comprehend the powerful formula behind the Amway business: the more people you help, the more you help yourself. You make money when they make money. You climb higher when they climb higher. Your ability to stand on your own and achieve financial independence is dependent on your commitment to helping others do the same. And so with total sincerity and proven results, a spirit of helping others infuses the thoughts, words, and deeds of Amway's most successful people.

Crown Ambassadors Dan and Bunny Williams believe the best thing that could ever be said about them is that they "brought love to the Amway business." INA Chairman and Executive Diamond Jim Elliott told me that "helping people is what attracted me to the Amway business." Executive Diamond Betty Kaufmann says that the greatest reward she and her husband, Pat, get out of the business is watching people "become."

Crown Ambassadors Paul and Debbie Miller of North Carolina have said that friends and neighbors were never quite convinced by their success in the business until "we started giving 10 percent of our income to our church and other offerings to the causes we believe in all around our community." Paul adds, "Don't wait to be generous until that time when you can afford it. Be generous now and be surprised at what you receive in return."

And Crown Ambassador Dexter Yager, who rose from a brewery sales and delivery job in Rome, New York, to become one of the most renowned success stories in the history of American entrepreneurship, has said, "Love is the glue that holds this business together. We build relationships—and people normally don't quit on people who love them."

* * *

Dexter Yager should know. In his darkest hour, he was sustained by the people who loved him—thousands of people whose lives he had made measurably better.

In the mid-1960s, Dexter and his wife, Birdie, were simply looking for a way out of the drudgery of their existence. Dexter's dreams focused on cars. His evening walks after work in Rome, New York, invariably took him to the Cadillac dealership downtown. "I stood there in the darkness," he recalled, "staring at the brightly lit Cadillacs in the showroom window. I focused on a light blue DeVille with plush leather seats and electric windows. We didn't have a dime extra in the bank, but standing in the darkness, I told myself over and over again that one day soon, that car would be mine."

Birdie's dreams turned to homes. "I dreamed that our children would have a backyard with a lawn and a little stream, on a street that was peaceful and safe," she has said.

So, in 1964, the Yagers took a chance on a still-new business that sounded fishy to many of their friends and relatives. Just ten weeks after they started, they won an Amway sales contest and a trip to Ada, Michigan, but Dexter's boss refused to let him take the time off to go. So he made one of the most important decisions in his life: he quit his job to build a business he could call his own.

* * *

"I learned to focus on what I wanted," Dexter remembers. "I had to claim my own life back from all those well-intentioned folks who thought their dreams for me were better than my own. Day after day, night after night, I fed on my dreams for the future."

Success through the seventies and eighties was spectacular. Dexter Yager's story became an entrepreneur's textbook legend, not just in the Amway world but beyond. The 1955 Ford station wagon and humble row house in upstate New York were replaced with a colonial-style mansion in Charlotte, North Carolina, and a fleet of priceless antique cars. The Yagers' business expanded to hundreds of thousands of distributors operating all over the world. Even Rich DeVos, no stranger to the kind of success Amway can generate, marvels that "five different American presidents had invited the former beer salesman and his wife to be their guests in the White House."

Most of Dexter and Birdie's seven children are active in the business. One of Dexter's favorite stories is about the time his daughter came home from college and told him, "Dad, my economics professor disagrees with everything you say—and he's broke!"

As the Yagers soared to the height of prosperity, they never forgot their roots, giving to a long list of charities and opening a children's camp that teaches the free enterprise system. Life was rich and rewarding on many levels.

Then, in October 1986, Dexter suffered a debilitating stroke. He was rushed to intensive care, paralyzed on his right side and unable to walk. Birdie received the bad news at the hospital: "The specialists warned me that if Dexter lived, he would never walk again. The family and

I gathered around his hospital bed. We were afraid that this proud and energetic man might be forced to lie there paralyzed and helpless until his death. The best we could hope for . . . was lifting Dexter in and out of a wheelchair for the rest of his life."

Dexter was haunted by the thought that he could no longer help people. "I had been rushing about the world for the past two decades caring for people that I loved. Now they would have to care for me."

An outpouring of love and emotion sustained Dexter as he lay in that hospital bed. It came in the form of thousands of cards, phone calls, and flowers from all over the world. Dexter made a vow. He would walk again. He would not listen to his doctors. He would lift himself up on the strength of the people he had made strong.

Rich DeVos sets the scene for us:

Late in 1988, a coliseum in North Carolina was filled with Dexter and Birdie's friends and coworkers. The plan was simple. Birdie would wheel Dexter onto the stage. He would wave his good arm, share a few words of encouragement, and then be wheeled off the stage again. . . .

Then Dexter appeared. He wasn't in his chair. He was walking. It was more of a step, drag, step, but he was walking. And the gloom lifted like a curtain. People's eyes filled with tears, not of grief but of joy and gratitude. Dexter was walking.

Dan Williams has known Dexter Yager for over 30 years. "Dexter was born a server," he told me. "It's the little things that you always remember. And I remember the time just a few years ago when Bunny and I were traveling to a meeting in Rio de Janeiro. As we struggled with our luggage at the airport, Dexter spotted us from a distance and rushed over to help us with our bags. Imagine that—after he had suffered a stroke. There were people all around us, but it was Dexter Yager who came over to help us. He is a born server, and the more you serve, the more you get."

* * *

As I reflected on Dan's observations, I thought about a headline I had seen recently on the front page of the May 17, 1996, issue of *USA Today:* "Clinton Urges CEOs to Share the Wealth." President Clinton's plea was just one of a long series of pronouncements to emerge recently from Washington, D.C. Secretary of Labor Robert Reich and House Minority Leader Richard Gephardt have made impassioned speeches urging "good corporate citizenship" and have mulled proposals to skew the tax code to encourage what they deem to be socially responsible behavior. From a different perspective, conservative leaders like Bob Dole have issued stern lectures to corporate Hollywood, appealing for sex- and violence-free entertainment.

Usually lost in the sermonizing from government is the fact that the American free enterprise system has created the most broadly based level of economic prosperity in human history. That's no small contribution to social responsibility!

For the people of Amway, from the corporation's founding families to the newest of distributors, the sermonizers from Washington, D.C., are merely preaching to the choir. The first gathering of Amway distributors I ever attended was a fund-raiser for Easter Seals organized by INA in Southern California. I wanted to talk to them about their business. They wanted to talk about Easter Seals.

Without a lot of fanfare, the Amway Corporation has tackled pressing social concerns in its own unique way, sometimes leading by example, always putting its money where its mouth is. Whether participating in global environmental efforts spearheaded by the United Nations or establishing an employee-pupil pen pal program with an elementary school down the street, the company has lived up to cofounder Rich DeVos's vision of a "compassionate capitalism."

* * *

Amway is a multibillion-dollar global company operating in more than 70 countries and territories. Its founders and other top leaders have been friends and confidants of presidents and kings and captains of industry. Yet, the company has never lost the neighborly spirit it embodied when it was just two guys and their wives toiling in their basements in a Grand Rapids suburb. What happens around the corner is just as important to the Amway team as what happens around the world.

Look at the impact in Grand Rapids, Michigan. Walk out the door of the Amway Grand Plaza Hotel in the city center and you are within eyesight of a $60 million Van Andel sports and entertainment arena. Down the street on the riverfront is the Van Andel Museum Center, a $39 million project to which Jay and Betty Van Andel contributed $6 million as well as 700 pieces from their collection of works by Michigan print artist Reynold Weidenaar. There's also the DeVos Hall, a center for the performing arts, and the Van Andel Living Shores Aquarium at the John Ball Zoo.

Sigsbee Elementary School is in a poor area of Grand Rapids. Eighty-eight percent of the kids come from so-called disadvantaged households. The Amway family up the street has "adopted" the school, creating a Partners in Education program to ensure that students learn basic skills, develop good personal habits, and progress with positive, hopeful attitudes. A pen pal program matches a Sigsbee student with an Amway employee. Similar programs have been duplicated by Amway distributors from California to Austria. The Grand Rapids Toys for Tots program has also benefited from Amway's beneficence. So has an orphanage in Indonesia and UNICEF in Brazil.

From scholarships sponsored through the United Negro College Fund to a chair in disease prevention endowed at Stanford University to generous support for Junior Achievement's programs to encourage economic literacy, education is a valued commodity in the Amway philosophy. Opportunity, not dependency, is the watchword.

Long before there was an Earth Day, long before there was an Environmental Protection Agency, Amway Corporation developed products and policies that are considerate to the environment. To paraphrase the country song, Amway was "clean" before "clean" was cool!

The very first product manufactured by the company was L.O.C. Multi-Purpose Cleaner—a liquid organic cleaner containing only biodegradable ingredients and no phosphates. In deference to the earth's sensitive ozone layer, Amway aerosol products switched to environmentally friendly propellants worldwide long before the imposition of an international ban on the more damaging propellants.

Amway's commitment to the environment has also been recognized by organizations not always known for their favorable assessments of business—particularly businesses engaged in manufacturing and associated with conservative politics. In 1989, Amway received the United Nations Environment Programme Award in honor of the company's commitment to environmental education among youth. The National Wildlife Federation recognized the corporation in 1991 for its varied and multifaceted conservation efforts.

Corporate giving is neither new nor unusual. Many companies endeavor to be good neighbors and solid corporate citizens. Yet the smell of pragmatism and public relations permeates many of these programs. As good as their intentions may be, salaried CEOs are, after all, giving away "other people's money"—the shareholders' money—often with the counsel of public relations firms who create "corporate giving strategies" for maximum public exposure. Of course, that's nothing compared to government, where elected officials routinely spend *our* tax money on public works and then put *their* names on the projects!

Amway dollars are real dollars—not "other people's money." From the distributor to the corporation, the millions of dollars donated to charities come directly out of the pockets of the people who actually earn it. It's hard-earned, real money that is gladly given.

Yet it's more than money. Amway has marshaled its entire business network in support of Easter Seals. From the restrictions the company placed on the use of animals in product development laboratory tests to its current experimentation to prevent repetitive motion injuries in the workplace (ergonomics), Amway has been ahead of its time—a leader in tackling pressing social issues. The company has proven that social consciousness is not incompatible with profits.

When all is said and done, however, it's the accessibility of the Amway business opportunity that constitutes the firm's greatest contribution to society. You don't need a fancy family background, high-level connections, or a batch of university degrees to take part. Your race, ethnicity, or religion won't hold you back.

A favorite line used in speeches defending private enterprise is "A rising tide lifts all boats." Amway's win-win formula for success has given life to that rhetoric. The more you help the people around you to succeed, the more you succeed. It's that simple. Triple Diamond Direct Distributor Brian Hays told me about a letter one of his downlines had received from a new distributor couple. The letter was plain-spoken and blunt. It said their family had fallen into serious financial trouble. They barely had enough money to feed their kids, but they had a part-time Amway business. "We don't make a lot of money from that business," they said. "But you know something? The small amount of money we do make has enabled us to buy lunch meat for children's sandwiches. The Amway income made all the difference as to whether we could send our children to school with a full lunch box."

In ways large and small, Amway and businesses like it are redefining the meaning of capitalism for people all around the world. We have been taught that as successful as it is in creating material abundance, the ethic of capitalism is still "dog eat dog." Amway is changing the way we think, not about the achievements of free enterprise, but about the spirit behind it. It's not dog eat dog. It's people helping people.

12

Moment of Truth

I really believe that people like us in this room tonight, and our offspring, will determine whether there's freedom in the world in the future.
— Crown Ambassador Bill Britt, at a Free
Enterprise rally in Norfolk, Virginia

I've never met the Dinh family of Springfield, Virginia, and for reasons of privacy I've been reluctant to contact them. I have no idea if they're part of Amway or if they even know what Amway is. But the Dinhs' story of survival, sacrifice, and perseverance, as told in the local media, reminds us all of just how fiercely the yearning for freedom burns in the hearts of men and women everywhere.

On May 17, 1996, the last of the Dinhs' six children graduated from the University of Virginia—the great university founded by the man who wanted to be known simply as the author of the American Declaration of Independence, Thomas Jefferson.

Six immigrant children, six degrees from the University of Virginia, and most of the tuition was paid for out of the family's savings.

Graduation day, 1996, seemed so far in space and time from April 30, 1975, the day Saigon fell to the communists. Through different treacherous routes—out of prisons, into leaky boats, into refugee camps—the Dinhs made their way to a new life of freedom in the United States. So, too, did a million other Vietnamese. Thousands died on the journey—blown up by land mines while walking across Cambodia, murdered by pirates in the Gulf of Thailand, drowned in storms in the South China Sea.

Life wasn't easy in America. Despite their professional backgrounds, Mr. and Mrs. Dinh worked, without complaint, in menial jobs in order to feed their family. They staggered their shifts so that one parent could be at home with the children. One by one, those children, with straight-A high school averages, got into the University of Virginia, made their parents proud, and made all the risk and sacrifice seem worthwhile.

Their father, Thuy Dinh, thinks it's no big deal. "A lot of people have lost faith in being able to succeed, like the old American Dream no longer exists," he says. "But if we can come over here with virtually nothing, if we were able to do it, I think other people can, too.

"You have to have a lot of faith and respect for one another, and then just go out and do what you have to do." The Dinhs never gave up on their dreams—and their dreams never gave up on them.

I *used* to think the Dinhs' story was remarkable and unique. It is indeed remarkable, but I have now learned that the most remarkable thing about it is that it is *not* all that unique. It repeats itself every day, in towns, cities, and farms across our country and around the world. The names change. The details vary. The skin colors and religions are different. The story remains the same. It is the story of Amway.

What's so ideal about the Amway opportunity is that, unlike the Dinh family, you don't have to set sail across a big ocean in a leaky boat to join. The business does not require you to leave your home, quit your job, or invest your life savings. All Amway asks and offers is that you begin a journey—a journey you'll share with others, benefiting from their friendship, support, and wise counsel. It is a journey you can make with your family by your side, a journey that can change your life.

House Speaker Newt Gingrich tells students in his History of American Civilization course that "in America, the freedom to be alone makes possible the freedom to join."

Americans are joiners. French writer Alexis de Tocqueville observed this quality in the brash, young America of the 1840s, and it's even more true today. We are free to stand alone and free to join—and because the choice is ours, we choose to join. Executive Diamonds Glen and Joya Baker discovered this about Amway and America, too. "We learned they were all going through the same things," Glen said of the other distributors in their group. "We pointed out to them that we were all in the same boat together, and we'd better all start rowing in the same direction."

As you make the decision to start your own business—to free yourself from the trap of working for someone else—you are becoming a "joiner" too. You are joining a movement that is historical in scope and global in reach. You are striking out on your own, but you are hardly alone.

This is a movement of people away from dependency on big government and big companies. It's a movement that celebrates the potential of the individual but at the same time nurtures that individual with support, training, friendship, and love. It's a movement that has glued broken families back together and reassembled shattered dreams. It crosses continents and cultures with breathtaking ease.

In America, you can see it in the dramatic increase in the self-employed: 15 million Americans are working for themselves. This calculates to 12 percent of the workforce, maybe as much as 17 percent.

You can see it happening around the world. There is no greater illustration than the rush of hopeful people to Amway's doors every time the company opens for business in a new country.

The dream is powerful, and the movement is growing, but the going is not always easy. A still-powerful array of interest groups, regulators, and tax collectors work overtime to impose additional burdens on entrepreneurs. In new markets overseas, Amway pioneers have also had to overcome formidable barriers imposed by skeptical and suspicious governments. They can all make the dreaming tough.

Winston Churchill said it best: "Some see private enterprise as a cow to be milked. Others see it as a target to be shot at. Few see it as the sturdy horse pulling the wagon." Amway offers you an opportunity (borrowing a phrase from Henry David Thoreau) to "hitch your wagon to a star."

This is a business movement that refuses to let the fog of negativism so prevalent today dampen our dreams.

A conversation was once overheard outside a classroom of one of our great universities. The student asked his teacher, "Do you mean to tell me that the freest, fairest, and most productive economic system known to mankind is based on private ownership and the profit motive?" The teacher said, "That's right; it's called free enterprise." The student replied, "But isn't there some solution to this?"

"Fold up your newspaper, turn off your television, tune out the negativism," wrote Jay Van Andel and Rich DeVos more than 20 years ago. It's wise counsel today.

Executive Diamonds Dave and Jan Severn believe that rejecting the voices of negativism is critical to success in the Amway business. "Never listen to the critics," Dave told me. "Just keep on going. That's the key."

The Severns speak from personal experience. Back in the late 1970s, Dave was a CPA and Jan worked as a receptionist for an insurance company. There was just one problem: "We were going broke at 100 miles per hour," Dave said. "We were just too stupid to know it."

They knew something had to change. Dave and Jan were working hard and playing by the rules. But they had no freedom and felt they had nothing to look forward to. Their marriage felt the strain.

The Severns were given a chance to take control of their lives when Dave's college roommate looked him up after 10 years and showed him the Amway Plan. But for the first six months, "we did nothing," Jan remembered. There was so much criticism, so much negativism, and the Severns listened to it.

Soon, however, they decided to tune it all out. With the strong, sure hand of Ron and Georgia Lee Puryear guiding them, the Severns' business grew. Seventeen months after they began, they were netting four times the income Dave received as a CPA.

On November 28, 1978—the date will be forever fixed in Dave's mind—he quit his job to devote full time to Amway. "We got in Amway to be free," Jan told me, and the Severns have now enjoyed freedom for more than 18 years. Amway has enabled them to shoulder some serious family medical expenses, set their own schedules, provide outstanding educational opportunities for their children, and divide their time between their estate in Spokane, Washington, and their ranch in Idaho.

"Amway has changed our lives," Dave said. "And that's the only way we'll ever change America—not from the top down, but the bottom up. That's what Amway is doing, not just here but all around the world."

Robert Angkasa, a Diamond from Indonesia, has a different approach: "A great pleasure in life is doing what other people say you can't do." He relates the time he was enjoying the beaches of Hawaii and sent postcards to all the negative people back home who had told him he'd never make it.

"I'm very thankful for those negative people," Robert says. "They motivate me a lot."

It was a long, long journey to those beaches. Robert recalls his upbringing in Indonesia. "I was the third of four children. I was not a special person.

"My father worked 40 years as an employee and received no recognition when he retired. When I saw this business, I thought it was really important for those who never got any recognition. I didn't want to end up like my father."

Robert traveled to Australia and put himself through school by working as a waiter, as a garbage collector, and at many other odd jobs. "Luck is spelled the same way in any language," he says. "It's spelled W-O-R-K."

He decided he wanted to be a corporate man and did pretty well at becoming one, eventually landing a good position with Citibank. He was introduced to the Amway business in Australia, but it was not until he learned that the business would soon open in his native Indonesia that he decided to go back home and build it.

Returning to his country in January 1992 to prepare for Amway's opening later in the year, Robert found nothing but discouragement. There were no brochures, no products, no business kits, and no educational materials. "People thought I was a con man," he recalls.

He beat a retreat back to the corporate world. Again, he did very well. "But my upline from Australia kept calling, and so I tried to do both—work at my job and build this business. I lived on four hours of sleep a night and learned to hate alarm clocks."

While managing inaugural activities in Indonesia for the Network 21 organization, Robert also encountered many difficulties with authorities. It was always a challenge to ensure that the proper permits were secured and all the rules followed. On more than one occasion, meetings had to be postponed and prospects sent away. "They kept coming back, and those who stuck with it have been successful."

Robert and his group now bring together thousands of people in over 75 cities in Indonesia to learn about the business. Poor people scratching together the money they need to travel to the meetings, sleeping in bus stations—all in search of their dreams.

"There are literally thousands of people in my country whose lives have been changed so much because of this business," Robert tells his American friends. "If we can do it in Indonesia, I'm sure you can do it, too."

For Robert Angkasa, the measure of his success is very simple: "I don't have alarm clocks anymore!"

Robert's story, like that of the Dinhs', is remarkable but not unique. He fought long odds, worked hard, and lifted himself above the fog of negativism.

On the surface, that shouldn't be so difficult to do, considering the splendid moment in history in which we live. Think about it: Marxism, not capitalism, lies on the ash heap of history. Richard Nixon's grandchildren do not live under communism; Nikita Khrushchev's grandchildren live in freedom. The Berlin Wall is gone—plucky entrepreneurs sold pieces of the rubble to souvenir seekers. The "Age of Entitlement" is quickly collapsing under the weight of its own flawed premise and fraudulent promise that with a shrug of the shoulders Americans would trade self-reliance for the deadening existence of cradle-to-grave government dependence.

Amid the ruins of these old empires, a new empire has taken hold. An empire of freedom. Two-and-a-half million Amway distributors from every corner of the world are its foot soldiers. Millions more will join their march into the twenty-first century.

It's an empire without walls. Its army has no guns. It seeks not to conquer but only to unshackle the unlimited and universal capacity of people to dream. No dream is too big, and no dream is too small, as long as you can stand on your own with your family by your side.

Are you ready to be a part of this movement? Are you prepared to unshackle your dreams and unleash your imagination? Are you willing to risk rejection and be subjected to criticism from the professional naysayers and lifelong cynics? Are you prepared to work hard and build your dream, brick by brick?

If your answer is yes, then you will become part of a historic business movement that is reshaping the global economy. You will become part of a business family that is spreading love and understanding to all peoples and cultures of the world. Join this business, and you will become a stakeholder in the greatest human experiment in history: a free enterprise system in which people prosper when they help others prosper.

I have poured my life into the advocacy of free enterprise, but I never truly understood it until now. Capitalism has always been a beautiful abstraction for me, worshipped from afar and kept at a nice, safe distance. I have lionized its practitioners while fearing to become one myself. If you're fearful too, I can understand that. But like me, I hope you have been able to draw sustenance from the everyday heroes of Amway described in this book. If they can do it, why not you?

The words of Triple Diamond Direct Distributor Cherry Meadows offer us some simple wisdom: "The biggest mistake anyone can make is knowing to do right, but not doing it. Too many people sit around wishing for something wonderful to happen, when they should be making it happen."

And something Dexter Yager once said keeps echoing in my mind as well: "A dream unrealized is a dream imprisoned by that enemy of all enemies—the fear of failure."

* * *

I knew all about the nuts and bolts of capitalism. I wanted to find its heart and soul. I found it. I hope you have, too.

Freedom. It's the most beautiful word in the English language or any language. The freedom to dream, the freedom to dare. The freedom to reach high and far without fear. With open, loving arms, the people of Amway stand ready to embrace you, as they have me.

Appendix:
Amway Code of Ethics

Amway's strong focus on ethics is evidenced by its Code of Ethics, which all distributors must agree to adhere to when joining the business. The Code is as follows:

As an Amway distributor, I agree to conduct my Amway business according to the following principles:

- I will make the "Golden Rule" my basic principle of doing business. I will always endeavor to do unto others as I would have them do unto me.
- I will uphold and follow the Rules of Conduct as stated from time to time in official Amway manuals and other literature, observing not only the letter, but also the spirit, of these Rules.
- I will present Amway products and the Amway business opportunity to my customers and prospects in a truthful and honest manner, and I will make only such claims as are sanctioned in official Amway literature.
- I will be courteous and prompt in handling any and all complaints, following procedures prescribed in official Amway materials for giving exchanges or refunds.
- I will conduct myself in such a manner as to reflect only the highest standards of integrity, honesty, and responsibility, because I recognize that my actions as an Amway distributor have far-reaching effects, not

only on my own business, but on that of other Amway distributors as well.

- I will accept and carry out the various prescribed responsibilities of an Amway distributor (and of a sponsor and a Direct Distributor when I progress to such levels of responsibility) as set forth in official Amway literature.
- I will use only Amway-authorized and produced literature concerning the Amway Sales and Marketing Plan and Amway products.

Sources

"Amway Asia Pacific Announces Election of New Officers and Regular Quarterly Dividend." *PR Newswire*, 17 January 1995.

"Amway Begins CD Rom–based Catalog Distribution." *Multimedia Business Report*, 5 May 1995, no. 17, vol. 4.

"Amway Begins Sales in China." *AP Worldstream*, 10 April 1995.

Amway Corporation. *Amagram*, January 1995; March 1995; September 1995–January 1996.

"Amway Corp. Opens Affiliate in Republic of Slovakia." AP *Worldstream*, 2 November 1994.

"Amway Explores New Media for Distributor Communications." *Business Wire*, 17 April 1995.

"Amway Japan Announces Successful Completion of Global Public Offering NYSE." *Business Wire*, 18 August 1994.

"Amway Opens Offices in Honduras, El Salvador, Chile." *Associated Press*, 7 February 1995.

"Amway Sales in Brazil Up by 1500 Percent." *Latin American Law and Business Report*, 31 May 1995, no. 5, vol. 3.

"Amway Says It Does Not Condone Rumors on P&G." *Reuters*, 28 August 1995.

Becker, Gary S. "The Numbers Tell the Story: Economic Freedom Spurs Growth." *Business Week*, 6 May 1996, p. 20.

Brownstein, Paul. "The New Politics of Going Solo." *Los Angeles Times*, 3 May 1996, p. 1.

Butterfield, Stephen. *Amway: The Cult of Free Enterprise*. Boston: South End Press, 1974.

Calabrese, Dan. "Amway's China Efforts Tempered by Realities." *Grand Rapids Business Journal*, 23 May 1994, vol. 12, no. 21, p. 2.

Calabrese, Dan. "Vietnam Yes, but Amway Won't Rush into Russia." *Grand Rapids Business Journal*, 14 February 1994, vol. 12, no. 7, p. 1.

"Challenging Japan's Sales Culture." *Institutional Investor,* 24 May 1994, pp. 23–24.

Conn, Charles Paul. *An Uncommon Freedom: The Amway Experience and Why It Grows.* New York: Berkley Books, 1982.

Conn, Charles Paul. *The Possible Dream: A Candid Look at Amway.* New York: Berkley Books, 1978.

Coulombe, Charles. "Global Expansion." *Success,* September 1994, pp. 18–21.

Deck, Cecilia. "Stepping Up to the Challenge." *Detroit Free Press,* 12 April 1993, p. 5F.

DeVos, Richard M. *Believe.* New York: Berkley Books, 1975.

DeVos, Richard M. *Compassionate Capitalism.* New York: Dutton, 1993.

Doebele, Justin. "Global Way." *Forbes,* 18 July 1994, p. 318.

do Rosario, Louise. "Pressing the Flesh." *Far Eastern Economic Review,* 27 April 1995, p. 67.

Eisenstodt, Gale, and Katayama, Hiroko. "Soap and Hope in Tokyo." *Forbes,* 3 September 1990, p. 62.

Evans, Mark. "Having Penetrated Several Asian Markets, Amway Corp Is Now Turning Attentions to China." *South China Morning Post,* 18 April 1994, p. 3.

Fromson, Brett D. "Amway's Asian Unit Is an Instant Hit." *Washington Post,* 16 December 1993, p. B17.

Grant, Linda. "How Amway's Two Founders Cleaned Up." *U.S. News & World Report,* 31 October 1994, p. 77.

Harman, Liz. "Amway Distributor Savors Victory in Breach of Contract Suit." *San Diego Business Journal,* 11 September 1995, p. 3.

Harris, David John. *Of Prophecy and Profit: A Study of the Amway Worldview.* Cambridge, Mass., Harvard University Archives (doctoral dissertation), 1992.

Hershey, Robert, Jr. "When Lifetime Jobs Die Prematurely." *New York Times,* 12 June 1996, D1.

Hoffman, Gary. "Amway Wraps Up Shaq Bar Deal with O'Neal." *The Detroit News,* 29 November 1995.

Hofheinz, Paul. "New Light in Eastern Europe." *Fortune,* 29 July 1991, p. 145.

Jones, Del. "Workers on the Edge." *USA Today,* 19 February 1996, p. 1B.

Kaskovich, Steve. "Steve Van Andel's Promotion Puts Amway in Hands of Next Generation." *The Detroit News,* 28 July 1995.

Klebnikov, Paul. "The Power of Positive Imagination." *Forbes,* 9 December 1991, p. 244.

Koretz, Gene. "China's Other Consumers." *Business Week,* 13 May 1996, p. 32.

"Laser Coding." *Packaging Digest,* August 1995, pp. 68–72.

Lesher, Richard L. *Meltdown on Main Street.* New York, Dutton, 1996.

MacGregor, Hilary E. "Job Outlook Is Bleak for Japan's Generation X." *Los Angeles Times,* 9 May 1996, p. A3.

Maney, Karen. "College Costs: Can Anyone Afford to Go?" *USA Today,* 15 April 1994, p. 4B.

March, Ann. "Amway Finds Eager Recruits in Czech Republic Launch." *Crain's Detroit Business,* 6 June 1994, p. I14.

McKay, David. "The Stamp of Benevolence." *Detroit Free Press,* 30 January 1995, p. 1A.

Morgan, Pat. "Amway to Restrict Tests on Animals." *Detroit Free Press,* 18 August 1989, p. 4B.

Muller, Joann. "Amway Sees Potential in Brazil's Volatile Economy." *Detroit Free Press,* 23 November 1991, p. 13A.

Muller, Joann. "Amway Will Peddle Wares in E. Europe." *Detroit Free Press,* 4 June 1990, p. 3F.

Mullich, Joe. "The Top 100; 63 Amway." *Crain Communications Business Marketing,* 1 October 1995, p. 34.

Naisbitt, John. *Megatrends Asia.* New York, Simon & Schuster, 1996.

"Notebook." *The New Republic,* 20 May 1996, p. 8.

Ono, Yumiko. "Amway Translates with Ease into Japanese." *Wall Street Journal,* 21 September 1990.

"Pacific Watch: Hong Kong." *Los Angeles Times,* 8 January 1996, p. D4.

Paton, Huntley. "The Amazing Money-Making Machine." *Business Journal of Charlotte,* 13 February 1995, vol. 9, no. 44, p. 1.

"Perfuming the Amazon." *The Economist,* 22 October 1994, p. 74.

Perlez, Jane. "A Bourgeois Blooms and Goes Shopping." *New York Times,* 14 May 1996, p. D1.

Perlstein, Steven. "For Richer, for Poorer: An Election-Year Primer." *Washington Post,* 5 May 1995, p. H1.

Peterson, Karen S. "Living in fear of a Layoff." *USA Today,* 2 May 1996, p. 1D.

Poe, Richard. "Wave 3." *Success,* June 1994, pp. 48–54.

Poe, Richard. *Wave 3: The New Era in Network Marketing.* Rocklin, Calif., Prima Publishing, 1993.

Quinn, Jane Bryant. "A Primer on Downsizing." *Newsweek,* 13 May 1996, p. 50.

Quinn, Jane Bryant. "Baby Boomers Should Plan for More Than an Inheritance." *Washington Post,* 23 August 1992, p.3.

Rudnitsky, Howard. "Ring, Ring, Jingle, Jingle." *Forbes,* 20 May 1996, p. 65.

Samuelson, Robert J. *The Good Life and Its Discontents: The American Dream in the Age of Entitlements.* New York, Random House, 1995.

"Sons of Amway Founders Assume Control of Company." *Orlando Sentinel,* 2 September 1995, p. C9.

"Steve Van Andel Appointed Amway Corp. Chairman" *Canada Newswire,* 27 July 1995.

Stewart, Thomas A. "How to Manage in the New Era." *Fortune,* 15 January 1990, p. 58.

Thatcher, Margaret. "The West after the Cold War." *Wall Street Journal,* 14 May 1995, p. A20.

Thornton, Emily. "Revolution in Japanese Retailing." *Fortune,* 7 February 1994, p. 143.

Timmermans, Jeffrey. "Amway Japan Pays Off for Holders." *Asian Wall Street Journal,* 6 November 1995, p. A23.

Troy, Tevi. "Downsizing: Myth and Reality." *Journal of Commerce,* 14 May 1996, p. 6A.

VanderVeen, Don. "New Market Explosions Ignite Amway." *Grand Rapids Business Journal,* 9 October 1995, vol. 13, no. 41, sec. A, p. 1.

Vanderveen, Don. "Amway, NBA Team Up for Vitamin Sales." *Grand Rapids Business Journal,* no. 35, vol. 12, p. 1.

"Where the Money Is." *Success,* December 1995, p. 31.

Wittstock, Melinda. "Multilevel Mission to Promote Enterprise." *Times of London,* 20 October 1989.

Wysocki, Bernard, Jr. "About a Million Men Have Left Work Force in the Past Year." *Wall Street Journal,* 12 June 1996, p. 1.

Wysocki, Bernard, Jr. "Early Retirement Isn't in the Boomers' Future." *Wall Street Journal,* 6 May 1996, p. 1.

Zachary, G. Pascal. "Major U.S. Companies Expand Efforts to Sell to Consumers Abroad." *Wall Street Journal,* 13, June, 1996, p. 1.

Other Inspirational Books from Prima

Family: Everyday Stories About the Miracle of Love

Samantha Glen
Mary B. Pesaresi

In the tradition of Chicken Soup for the Soul

U.S. $18.00

Family is a beautiful gift collection of 60 real-life, inspirational stories that celebrate the meaning of family. Contributed by ordinary people, young and old, these stories remind us of what is most important in life and all the precious wisdom and support that families provide for their members. A timely and important book, *Family* is a powerfully uplifting testimony to humanity's best qualities, celebrating the goodness in each of us.

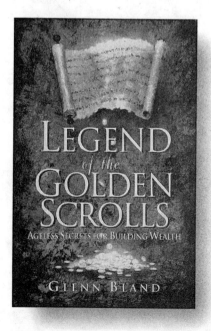

Legend of the Golden Scrolls: Ageless Secrets for Building Wealth

Glenn Bland

U.S. $12.00

Author Glenn Bland tells a fascinating tale of wealth, wisdom, and enlightenment by focusing on one man's search for the secrets of building wealth. This book contains an inspiring mixture of finely honed storytelling and wise practical advice.

Success Secrets of the Motivational Superstars: America's Greatest Speakers Reveal Their Secrets

Michael Jeffreys

U.S. $16.00

This one-of-a-kind collection features interviews with sought-after leaders such as Anthony Robbins, Wayne Dyer, Les Brown, Tom Hopkins, Barbara De Angelis, Art Linkletter, Brian Tracy—and many more! Millions who attend their seminars will find this book invaluable.

7 Strategies for Wealth & Happiness: Powerful Ideas from America's Foremost Business Philosopher

Jim Rohn

U.S. $12.00

In this remarkable book, Jim Rohn shows readers how to achieve financial freedom and richer, happier lives with his Seven Keys to Success and his time-tested, positive approach to personal success. This is a book that will continue to change lives for many years to come!

Selling for People Who Hate to Sell: Everyday Selling Skills for the Rest of Us

Brigid McGrath Massie with John Waters

U.S. $12.00

Written for so-called "non-sales-people," this is a powerful resource for anyone who wants to improve his or her performance and marketability in a highly competitive workplace. A book for anyone who wants to stay sharp and competitive in an uncertain world.

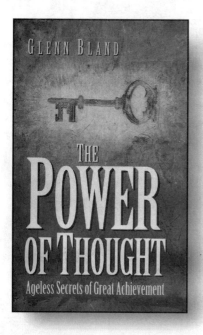

The Power of Thought: Ageless Secrets of Great Achievement

Glenn Bland

U.S. $16.95

Inspirational speaker Glenn Bland has studied examples of successful people in order to understand their common underlying characteristics and beliefs. This book discusses the importance of developing qualities such as trust, dreams, purpose, effort, and character.